Towards a sustainable economy

The world economy has devastated the lives of millions of
innocent people, it has been transferring resources systematically
from poor countries to rich countries, and it is destroying
the earth.

James Robertson, *Future Wealth*, 1990, p68.

OTHER BOOKS BY TED TRAINER

Dimensions of Moral Thought, Sydney, University of New South
  Wales Press, 1982
Abandon Affluence!, London, Zed Books, 1985
Developed to Death, London, Green Print, 1989
Development Economics, Melbourne, Heinemann, 1989
The Nature of Morality, Aldershot, Avebury, 1991
The Conserver Society, London, Zed Books, 1995
The Global Crisis, Sydney, Critical Social Issues Project, 1995

Towards a Sustainable Economy

The need for fundamental change

Ted Trainer

JON CARPENTER / OXFORD
ENVIROBOOK / SYDNEY

1166108 9

First published jointly in 1996 by
Envirobook, 88 Cumberland Street, Sydney, NSW 2000, Australia
and
Jon Carpenter Publishing, PO Box 129, Oxford OX1 4PT, England

Distributed in the USA and Canada by
Login Publishers Consortium, 1436 West Randolph Street, Chicago,
Ill 60607

ISBN 0 85881 141 3 (in Australia)
1 897766 14 9 (in the UK and North America)

Printed and bound in England by Biddles Ltd, Guildford and King's Lynn

Contents

Introduction

ANYONE WITH THE slightest interest in social issues should realise that the functioning of our economic system is not at all satisfactory. The conventional view is that although considerable change might be needed to make the system work well again, it does not require radical change. This book argues that our economic system and conventional economic theory are fundamentally mistaken and that both must be largely scrapped.

These issues are of enormous importance. The flaws in our economy must take most of the responsibility for the huge problems now threatening the globe such as mass poverty and hunger, underdevelopment, waste, unemployment, resource scarcity, environmental destruction and armed conflict. The problems are not inevitable; they could be avoided if sensible arrangements and systems were developed. But the present economic system is leading us in the opposite direction. It is increasingly becoming understood that a just, peaceful and safe world order cannot be achieved unless we develop a quite different economic system.

For 150 years the general Marxist critique of capitalism has focused on problems to do with power, inequality, distribution and consumption. Where this book differs from most critical analyses of the economy is in its analysis from a 'limits to growth' perspective; that is, in assessing the performance and prospects of our economy mainly in terms of its impact on the resource and ecological limits of our planet. Not only is our economy not solving our problems, it cannot permit us to move towards the less extravagant and wasteful lifestyles that are essential if an ecologically sustainable society is to be achieved.

The final chapter outlines the emerging alternative which includes some of the best elements of the two main economic systems that have functioned in the world, 'free enterprise capitalism' and 'big state socialism', but constitutes a Third Way, the economy of a radical conserver society. In view of the rapidly accelerating global environment and Third World crises, there is hardly any greater need than for contributions to the development of an economic theory and practice which enable us to build an ecologically sustainable and just world order.

Unfortunately, little of the recent literature on the quest for a new economics is reflected in the media or in public discussion. Consequently we have the tragic phenomenon of billions of people in both rich and poor countries doggedly plodding on through decaying social and natural landscapes towards a number of global catastrophes, without any understanding that none of this is necessary or that there are highly satisfactory alternatives.

There are few if any introductory accounts of these issues and it is hoped that this book will help to meet this need.

I

Overview

THE BASIC PROBLEM with our economy is that while it has enormous productive capacity and could easily provide all that people require, it fails to meet the needs of huge numbers of people or does so in an extremely wasteful way. There are many situations where we have the technical or productive capacity to provide what humans need yet we do not do this. For example, consider some of the contradictions surrounding hunger. The world produces more than enough food to feed everyone and most poor countries produce more food than they need. Nevertheless:

• At least 300 million and possibly 1000 million people do not get enough to eat, including over 20 million in the United States.

• More than half of the best land in the Philippines, a country with many hungry people, is used to grow crops for export.

• Cattle are air-freighted into Colombia, another hungry country, fattened on the best land, then transported to the US to be consumed in hamburger chains.

• The European Union has such huge mountains of surplus agricultural produce that billions of dollars are spent every year just for storage.

• One third of the world's grain, fish meal and milk powder is fed to animals in rich countries.

• In 1983 the United States government paid farmers $18 billion to keep 39 per cent of all cropland out of production.

Why? How can we explain these and other stunning contradictions in our economic system? These contradictions are not accidental. They are direct and inevitable consequences of the economic system we have.

The problems generated

In our economy, the projects in which capital is invested and the things that are to be produced are determined by what those who hold most capital think will make most money for themselves. They are free to set up factories to produce and sell whatever they think will maximise the return on their invested capital. Such a free enterprise or market economy has a number of important merits. Over the 300 years for which it has been dominant it has made an outstanding difference to the human situation, especially as it is very effective in harnessing human energy to production, stimulating change and new technologies, and in raising efficiency and levels of output. However, the same forces have strong tendencies to produce highly undesirable effects. This book's main purpose is to make clear that our most worrying global problems are directly due to an economy driven by market forces, the freedom of enterprise, the profit motive and the quest for endless economic growth. Here are some of the arguments that will be detailed later.

¤ *Scarce resources go to the relatively rich, because they can bid more for them.* Hence the one fifth of the world's people in rich countries get most of the oil and other resources, many of them produced in the Third World. Hundreds of millions of people suffer serious deprivation because the global market economy enables the few who are richer to take resources in their area, including land. It will be explained in Chapter 7 that there is no possibility of solving Third World problems until we change to an economy in which we produce what humans need, rather than what is most profitable to those with capital.

¤ *Because the most profitable things are produced, often things needed by large numbers of poorer people are not produced.* In other words, there is a strong tendency for the wrong industries to be developed, especially in the Third World, where the few with capital can make much more profit setting up factories to produce for the rich and for export to rich countries.

¤ *Inequality and poverty are extensive and becoming worse even in the richest countries.* The economy can be 'healthy' without employing everyone and without supplying what poorer people want. Over time there is a strong tendency towards increase in the numbers for whom this economy does not provide well.

¤ *Unemployment tends to increase all the time because this economy does not share the available work between all who want work and incomes.* Over time, technical advances increase the amount that can be produced per worker, meaning that there is a constantly increasing inability to employ all the available workers. Those with capital are free to employ people if and when they want them.

¤ *There is enormous but unavoidable waste.* Levels of resource use, work and productive activity in the economies of the rich countries are far higher than they would be in a sensible economy. We have vast quantities of totally unnecessary products, throw-away items and things not made to last or to be repaired. There is an enormous amount of driving to work and delivering of products which could be avoided by more sensible distribution of work places and farms. Yet we have an economy that cannot be healthy unless we not only keep up, but constantly increase the amount of production and consumption going on! Similarly, people feel a constant pressure to scurry around to find something to work at, produce or sell or they cannot earn a living, even though we do not need anywhere as much production as we have now.

¤ *There is inappropriate development.* In rich and poor countries this economy produces a great deal of development. Factories, roads, hotels and the like are being built all the time. However, many of these developments do not contribute to the production of the most needed things. In the Third World almost all development is inappropriate in view of what most people need. Even in the rich countries where, for instance, many people need cheap housing, investment does not go into such appropriate purposes. This is because investment goes into those areas that are most profitable. One consequence is that suburbs have not been developed to be economically and socially self-sufficient, ecologically sustainable or supportive communities.

¤ *Large numbers of people suffer boredom, loneliness and frustration.* Top priority is put on constantly increasing economic turnover rather than on developing communities that will provide all with worthwhile work, enjoyable and supportive surroundings and a high quality of life. In this economy many are deprived of adequate incomes, but more important is the emphasis it puts on privacy, competition, acquisitiveness, passive consuming and market relations, all of which tend to drive out community and meaningful and satisfying social relations. (See Chapter 8.)

◻ *This economy makes us do far too much work and producing.* If we lived more simply (without depriving ourselves of anything that matters), cut out most of the waste production going into advertising and throw-away items, and re-designed our settlements to require far less transport, energy etc., we could probably have highly satisfactory lifestyles on as little as one third or less of the present levels of production and work. (See Chapter 12.)

◻ *We are rapidly damaging the ecological life support systems of the planet.* The basic cause of the environmental impact is all the producing and consuming going on, using up scarce resources such as forests, and causing problems like the greenhouse effect through the resulting pollution. The only way to solve several of these problems is by drastically reducing the amount of producing and consuming going on. Yet we have an economy which has to have constant increase in production and consumption.

◻ *Growth is crucial in this economy.* The supreme goal is a constant increase in national output and in individual 'living standards', despite the great wealth and the high incomes of the richest countries. There is no point at which people would be considered rich enough or the GNP high enough or living standards good enough. There is no point at which we would have had sufficient development. This is because the economy is driven by the ceaseless quest for profitable investment outlets on the part of those who have capital. As they make profits their capital grows and it is not possible for them to invest it all profitably unless an increase in the value of producing and consuming takes place. Unless the total volume of output increases by at least 2 per cent p.a. (the rate at which productivity is increasing and therefore reducing the need for workers) unemployment will grow.

Yet many people are now arguing that we are encountering the 'limits to growth'. They insist that the pursuit of economic growth in a world where there are resource and environmental limits is rapidly generating serious global problems, such as the greenhouse effect. Chapter 5 will outline their argument that our society is grossly overdeveloped and unsustainable.

◻ And we are now going backwards! Thirty years ago the rich countries were producing more than would have been enough to provide high material living standards to all people. Now they are producing 2–3 times as much per capita, yet they are not eliminating poverty, some of their real average wage levels are falling, and their debt, unemployment and social problems are definitely much worse. Making the growth of business turnover and GNP the supreme goal has generated far more wealth, but it has not solved any of the important problems. People can buy more but the evidence indicates that their quality of life is probably lower, and falling. If we were able to devote our energies directly to building a good society we could surely provide all that is necessary for a very satisfactory material living standard and very comfortable, secure and rewarding social arrangements on a small fraction of the present levels of work, production and resource use. Yet here we are, condemned to work frantically and strive to increase production all the time, while our quality of life, social conditions and ecological systems deteriorate. How long will it take to grasp that we are on the wrong path?

Many people, writing from various perspectives over recent years, have contributed to this general critical view of our economy. This economy has reached a stage in its evolution where its problems have become very serious. It is not providing at all well for most of the world's people and it has powerful tendencies to increasingly ignore and deprive most people. Chapter 5 will argue that there is no possibility of the system providing present rich world living standards for all. It is squandering the world's scarce resources on the rich few, and above all it is now consuming the earth's precious energy, mineral and especially biological capital at such an alarming rate that we have only a few decades in which to change to a radically different system.

Nevertheless, the conventional view of the economy remains so dominant that most economists, politicians, bureaucrats and ordinary people have no doubt that even though the economic system has obvious and major problems, there is no need to change from an economy driven by market forces, the freedom of enterprise, the profit motive and the quest for growth.

The alternative?

When the magnitude and urgency of our 'limits to growth' problem is grasped it is clear that the only viable long-term solution is to move to an economic system which provides satisfactory living standards on far lower per capita levels of production and consumption than we have now. This means a more simple, self-sufficient and cooperative way of life, and not just eventually a zero-growth economy, but in the short term moving to much lower levels of production, consumption and GNP per capita than we have now in rich countries.

Our present economy cannot possibly allow us to move in the required direction! It can be 'healthy' only if production and consumption rise by more than 3 per cent annually. There is no possibility of solving the limits to growth problem unless we change to a very different economic system.

Many of the problems noted above point to the need for considerable social control over the economy. Many vitally important things will not be done unless we deliberately plan and organise to do them. But as Chapter 12 will make clear, the solution is emphatically not the big-state variety of socialism where huge, centralised and inaccessible bureaucracies make the decisions, often in a dictatorial and inefficient way. A 'Third Way' is now being advocated. It involves some of the best elements of the free enterprise and the socialist ways but it is very different from both. The essential theme is a much simpler economy, highly localised, whereby small regions largely meet their own economic needs in basically cooperative and participatory ways with little need for bureaucracy, giant corporations, international importing or exporting or large state governments. We would have local control over most development, via town meetings and by the key role our town bank and its elected board would play in deciding local investment priorities. There would be many small local firms mostly using local resources to meet local needs. The new economy would have large sectors devoted to cooperatives, barter, gifts, voluntary labour and free goods. The cash economy would be a relatively minor part of a sustainable or conserver society, whereas in capitalist societies it is overwhelmingly dominant.

Most people would only need quite low cash incomes and would therefore only need to work one day a week at a normal job in the cash sector. The overall volume of producing and consuming would be much lower than it is now, because we would be living more simply and because the more sensible organisation of settlements and systems would have eliminated the need for much of the production carried out now, such as producing trucks to bring food to where people live. The economy would cease to be such an important aspect of society, because we would easily produce the relatively simple goods and services necessary. We would therefore be able to devote most of our attention to the non-economic matters that are far more important, such as cultural activities, arts and crafts, community development, personal growth and simply enjoying life.

These are huge changes, but they would not be difficult to make if most people were in favour of them, since they do not require large amounts of capital or difficult infrastructure development. Many communities throughout the world already function more or less according to these principles. The difficulty lies in getting most people in the mainstream to understand that such changes must be made if we are to achieve anything like a sustainable and satisfactory world order.

2

Market forces, free enterprise and the profit motive

IN ORDER TO understand how the present economy generates the problems mentioned in Chapter 1, we must first briefly note the essential characteristics of the system.

How our economic system works

¤ *Most capital or productive capacity (e.g. mines and factories) is owned by a few individuals,* not by the society as a whole.

¤ *Capital is put into production in order to make as much profit as possible.* Production is not undertaken in order to meet human needs.

¤ *There is freedom of enterprise.* Those who own the capital are allowed to invest it in what they like and workers are free to work for whom they choose. People are free to buy what they wish. Although it is far from a purely free enterprise economy, governments are in general concerned to leave as much economic activity as possible to private enterprise.

¤ *The basic assumption is that the welfare of all is best served when those with capital seek to maximise their incomes by maximising production and sales.* It is assumed that the more economic turnover there is, the more production there is of the things people want.

¤ *Market forces are allowed to determine supply, demand, investment and distribution.* What is to be produced is not determined by public discussion of what is necessary or sensible. If the demand for something increases then the price increases and people who own factories will produce more of it.

¤ *Economic growth is crucial;* the system can't work for long without it. Unless those with capital can expect to get back more than they invest they will not continue to invest. By reinvesting their constantly increasing wealth they continually expand the productive capacity of the economy. In addition technical advance is always reducing the need for labour, so unless the total consumption of output doubles every 20 years or faster, unemployment must grow.

¤ *The system's driving force is accumulation,* i.e. the determination to make profits, which can be invested in order to make more profits, to invest... in an endless spiral. This drive has been the most important factor shaping our society's history and its present form.

The major faults in our economy can be explained fairly simply in terms of the above characteristics.

Hence the basic faults

The most fundamental of all contradictions in our economic system is between market forces and the profit motive on the one hand, and what humans need on the other. If we allow the quest for most profit within a free market to determine what will be produced and how it is distributed, then the outcome will not be the one most desirable in view of the needs of people. People differ a great deal in their purchasing power, or 'effective demand'; i.e. in the amount of money they have to spend. Those who have capital to invest are not going to make much money setting up factories to produce the things poorer people need when they can produce and sell things richer people want. Consider housing for instance. It is quite possible to build a perfectly adequate house for less than A$15,000 (£9,000 or US$11,000).[1] But no corporation is interested in doing this when there is a huge demand for large and expensive houses. It is usually far more profitable to produce things middle- and high-income people want.

Another way of putting this is to say that market forces will always allocate scarce things to richer people. It does not matter how great a person's need is; if others can bid more they will get the desired goods.

There can be important benefits in allowing market forces to determine the distribution of goods and investment priorities. However, it is no exaggeration to say that the world's most serious problems are due to market forces. This is simply because market forces and the profit motive are appallingly bad at distributing goods

or investment according to human need, and this explains the
following extremely serious faults and injustices glaringly evident in
the world.

1. THE RICH COUNTRIES GET MOST OF THE WORLD'S RESOURCES

The one fifth of the world's people who live in the rich countries use
up at least 75 per cent of available resources at a per capita average
rate which is about 17 times that at which the poorest half of the
world's people consume them. This is because the rich countries can
obtain most of the resources by outbidding everyone else. The
average person in a rich country uses about 14 barrels of oil a year,
while the average Ethiopian uses only 1/13th of a barrel. As a result,
millions of Ethiopians have to drink dangerously dirty water, unable
to afford the fuel to sterilise it, while people in rich countries can run
cars and ski boats.

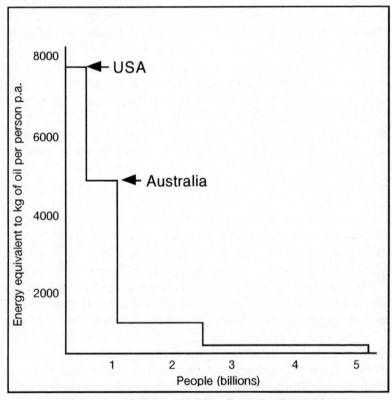

Fig 2.1: World Energy Use. Distribution 1988

2. THE WRONG INDUSTRIES ARE BEING DEVELOPED IN THE THIRD WORLD

There is now a great deal of development taking place in the Third World but most of it is development of the wrong things. Third World people need more cheap food, clothing and shelter, basic medical services and a clean water supply. Instead, luxury hotels and consumer goods factories are being developed at the expense of industries that could produce what the poor majority need. Why? Because it is far more profitable to set up a factory or plantation to produce for the rich few, especially those overseas in developed countries, than to produce what poor local people need.

3. MANY PEOPLE IN EVEN THE RICHEST COUNTRIES MUST GO WITHOUT WHAT THEY NEED

It has been estimated that one-fifth of Australia's children were living in poverty in the mid-1980s. More cheap housing, more hospitals and better public transport are urgently needed but resources which could have built these are diverted to provide luxury housing and fast food outlets.

Why? Because it is far more profitable to produce the many relatively unnecessary luxury goods that more affluent people will buy. If the most necessary industries were to be developed there would have to be some degree of deliberate rational planning *contrary* to what market forces and profit would urge. In addition, many investments which would be very profitable (such as relatively expensive housing) would have to be *prevented* so that these resources could be invested in what most needs doing.

'But isn't economic theory based on the fact that the invisible hand of the market is the best mechanism for making production and investment decisions?' This basic conventional principle assumes a short-run situation in which there is no serious inequality. If all people had equal 'effective demand' the market might distribute things among them satisfactorily, but in the real world there is very great inequality and most people cannot bid against those who are more wealthy.

In historical perspective we can see that economies driven by market forces and the profit motive have achieved wonders. They freed productive capacity from the feudal arrangements blocking economic progress and generated enormous productive capacity.

For a long time these forces contributed greatly to the improvement of human welfare (although they also devastated the welfare of many). However, *the profit motive and market forces have now become the greatest obstacles to human progress.* They still do some things well, but there is less and less tendency for the most profitable ventures to be those most likely to satisfy urgent needs. The problems generated by profit and the market, such as inequality, waste, environmental destruction and unemployment, have become so serious that we are threatened with major social and ecological breakdown within coming decades.

Our future depends primarily on whether or not we can shift to an economic system in which we are able to ensure that necessary, sensible production and development decisions are taken rather than the most profitable ones. Establishing appropriate limits and guidelines for the profit motive and the freedom of enterprise is of course quite a difficult task. There are great dangers in the other extreme; i.e., a heavy handed, 'big-state', planned socialist economy. (That is not the option advocated in Chapter 12.)

A major merit claimed for the existing economy is that the profit motive and competition in the market maximise efficiency. There is no doubt that they do provide very effective incentives for firms to cut costs, and they can restructure an economy quickly by eliminating weak and clumsy firms and prompting new developments when new demands arise. Alternative economic systems, especially centrally planned socialist systems, tend to be far less efficient in these respects. But as has been explained, when it comes to meeting human needs the profit motive and market forces are extremely inefficient. How efficient is a global food system which produces far more food than all the world's people need but annually feeds half a billion tonnes of grain to animals in rich countries, and grows luxury crops for export from many of the hungriest countries, while hundreds of millions of people are hungry? It is the market and the profit motive which devote the best Third World land to export crops and pay starvation wages to those who work in the export plantations. Efficiency is defined only in terms of minimising the dollar costs of whatever is produced. But this is not the most important question; what matters most is whether the right things are produced and distributed in the right ways.

It is often said that you can't expect firms to produce what very poor people need because these people could not afford to pay enough to meet production costs. Yet it is almost always possible to produce and sell at low prices the things that are most needed while still making a small profit. For example, in the late 1980s the cost of producing a barrel of oil in the Middle East was only about 50c, meaning that oil could be sold profitably to poor countries thought the world at far less than the $34 a barrel the rich nations have been prepared to pay in recent years.

The market is the direct cause of the world's most serious problems of deprivation and inappropriate development. In Chapter 12 it will be argued that market forces and free enterprise could play an important role in a sustainable economy but they could not be allowed to be anywhere near as dominant as they are now.

NOTE

1 Trainer, F.E., *The Conserver Society; Alternatives for Sustainability*, Zed Books, London, 1995.

3

Waste: unnecessary work and resource use

OURS IS AN extraordinarily wasteful economy — but it has to be! If the economy were only to produce sufficient for a high quality of life for all, GNP would be much lower than it is now. It cannot possibly maintain the present level of GNP, or increase this each year, unless the amount of unnecessary production and consumption is maintained or increased.

It is difficult to understand why people in general fail to rebel at the huge amount of production and therefore resource use and work that takes place in this economy but which could be avoided. Here are some of the areas in which waste is glaringly evident.

¤ We buy and consume much more than we need for materially satisfactory living. This includes the expensive leisure habits we have developed, especially travelling overseas (instead of enriching the places where we live so that they are interesting places in which to spend most of our leisure time).

¤ Many of the things we do need are only available in unnecessarily elaborate or expensive forms. Sometimes the price of a simple but sufficient product, such as a home, could probably be one-fifth or less of the price of the current products on sale. Included in this category is unnecessary packaging.

¤ Few things are made to last or to be repaired and many things are made in throwaway form. The multiples here can be quite big. For example a milk bottle is used about 17 times on average, whereas a carton is only used once.

¤ Many of the systems we have involve very high and avoidable resource and labour costs. For example, we produce food far from cities and then have to package and transport it. Most people have to travel long distances to work. Instead of recycling wastes such as sewage, we have expensive systems for getting rid of them. We also have a vast advertising industry, which on the global level spends hundreds of billions of dollars every year in an effort to get us to buy more things. Almost all of that huge amount of work and resources would be saved in a sane economy.

◻ Then there is all the work that has to be done to fix damage caused by all the unnecessary work being done. For example we have to mend the roads worn out by the trucks carrying goods we could well do without.

◻ Similarly, a lot of work has to be done to care for people damaged because this society devotes most of its resources to producing profitable things rather than to building supportive and pleasant communities. A large proportion of our mental institutions, social workers, courts, therapists, police and care institutions would not be needed in a more sane economy.

Adding to all these items, and to the production costs of necessities, are profits and interest payments. At least 10 per cent — and probably 20 per cent — of the amount we pay goes to lenders and shareholders as the return on their investment. These are huge additions to the work people have to do to pay for things, and they would be avoided in a sensible economy.

The total magnitude of the unnecessary work and production in this economy is astounding. Next time you are stuck in a traffic jam just reflect on the proportion of the cars in view carrying people unnecessary distances to work at producing things we could do without, burning fuel carried half way around the world in ships that need not have been built, and reflect on the many trucks carrying goods that are not necessary and food that could have been grown locally, and on the hospitals we would not need if there were fewer accidents because there were fewer of those cars and trucks on the roads, etc.

Many of the items we do need are produced in unnecessarily expensive ways. Many items are far more luxurious than they need to be, especially cars and houses. Food is necessary but it is produced in ways that use vastly more energy than is necessary. Then there is all the infrastructure development that goes into building the factories and roads to produce the unnecessary items, and the work that has to go into repairing the damage all this unnecessary production causes.

Chapter 12 will set out the sort of economy many people are

saying we must move to if we are to solve global problems such as
resource waste and environmental damage. It is very likely that in
such an economy we could live very well, indeed enjoying life more
than we do in this society, on a small fraction of the work and
resource use we now have to engage in. Some people who live simply
in relatively self-sufficient communities only need about 10 per cent
or less of an average cash income. Some people believe we could
easily cut the overall amount of work by 50 per cent and cut the
GNP by 90 per cent.

This is one of the most powerful arguments for change to a
different economic system. The present system makes us all work far
more and produce far more and use far more resources and therefore
do far more environmental damage than we have any need to. We
could be devoting most of our lives to other things than production,
such as to arts and crafts, to exploring and learning, to community
development and to personal development, rather than to working
in boring factories.

> '...it is probably an understatement to identify about half of US
> production as wasteful, as serving no useful purpose.'
> D. Dowd, *The Waste of Nations*, London, Westview, 1989, p2.

But massive waste is essential in this economy!

It is totally impossible to reduce, let alone eliminate the vast amount
of waste in this economy. Indeed the waste must constantly increase
or economic chaos threatens. Nothing is more important in this
economy than that the total volume of production and sales should
constantly increase. There is no possibility of doing this if we only
produce the things people need for a good material living standard.
This means that we must not only go on consuming all the unnecessary and luxurious and throwaway trash we now produce, but that we
must produce and consume at least 3 per cent more of it every year!

Just imagine what would happen if we decided to stop producing
non-necessities such as speedboats and hair driers. The economy
would collapse. There would be a vast increase in unemployment
and bankruptcies. So we have to work a 35 or 40 hour week when
20 or even 10 might do, and rich countries have to use up far more
than their fair share of the world's resources (at least 17 times the per
capita consumption that half the world's people average) just to keep
this economy going!

The only way we can cure recession, even in the richest countries, is to crank up production and consumption as much as possible, even though these countries are already over-consuming the world's scarce resources. No one cares what new things are produced, so long as production and consumption keep rising.

The 'limits to growth' argument (see Chapter 5) is that we cannot solve the many serious global problems threatening us unless we move to far lower levels of production and consumption. Yet our present economy simply cannot allow us to do that. There is therefore no possibility of solving those problems unless we change to a very different economy, i.e. one that will enable us to produce just those small amounts of things we need for good living standards, with the lowest possible amount of work and resource use.

Significant contributions to this goal of keeping consumption high and rising are made by debt, advertising, and military spending.

Debt: crucial to keep factories going

The USA's total debt in 1985 was over $8,000,000,000,000. This is the value of all the producing and consuming that people have engaged in without being able to pay for it. In other words, if the people had been unable to borrow money and buy things on credit, their economy could only have sold $8 trillion less than it did sell, representing about two years' output from the whole economy. Note that interest must be paid on this debt. Some estimates indicate that on average people in Australia, the USA, Canada and Germany might be working between half and one day a week just to pay the interest on debt. This is one of the largest categories of unnecessary work and resource use that would be avoided in a sane economy. (See Chapter 9.)

Advertising

Our economy not only accepts advertising as normal and legitimate but as playing a vital role in keeping the economy 'healthy'. However, consider the absurdity of spending money to persuade people to consume things they would not have bought otherwise. The developed countries produce and consume far more than is needed for comfortable lifestyles, yet we have a vast industry spending more than $100,000,000,000 every year just to get people to buy and consume even more! In a sane economy there would be almost no effort put into persuading people to buy. There would be a small amount of informative 'advertising', such as letting people know about a concert, or some new item available. Cheap ways of spreading such information would be developed; for example, someone thinking of buying a new fridge might go to the local library to look up information on types available, or access such information by computer.

Advertising involves an enormous waste of resources and talent, yet it is an industry that is essential for making our present economy work. In a world where three billion people are very poor and many are so deprived of basic needs that at least 40,000 die unnecessarily every day, wasting resources on advertising is an obscenity.

Conclusions

This chapter has dealt with one of the most powerful yet generally overlooked arguments for fundamental economic change. The present economy makes us work 5 days a week, using huge quantities of resources and generating serious environmental damage, when most of that effort produces things we would not need if we were to live with simple but sufficient standards and to organise more sensible systems for living. But despite what might be three times as much work and producing as would suffice, in even the richest countries one-quarter or more of the people must go without material things they need and many more have an unsatisfactory quality of life.

Another way of putting this absurd situation is in terms of the pressure everyone feels to find a job, i.e. to produce something, because unless you do this you cannot get money to acquire the things you need. But we are far past the point where it is necessary for all available workers to toil for 35–40 hours a week at producing the goods and services required to provide a satisfactory lifestyle for all. Nevertheless people struggle desperately to produce and sell things few people want and people push themselves to do courses in the hope of getting one of the scarce jobs. This is the main reason why individuals and corporations go on doing evil things like building weapons and clearing forests; because in this economy they must find something more to produce, or be trashed. We are all trapped in a system that obliges us to do far more work and to use far more resources and to have far more environmental impact than would be necessary if we had an economy which allowed us to produce only what is sufficient for modest but satisfactory living standards.

4

Growth and trickle down

No COMMITMENT IS more firmly built into the foundations of our economy than growth. The conventional economic theorist cannot doubt that it is most important to strive for continual increase in production and sales. If economic growth is occurring, this is taken to mean that there is increase in the production and purchase of things people want. Hence, it is assumed that to increase the overall volume of output, the GNP, is to increase national wealth and living standards.

There is no choice about it, this economy *must* have growth. Unless there is at least a 3 per cent per annum increase in the volume of sales and consumption, our economy is in trouble. Unemployment rises and firms go bankrupt. Yet in countries like Australia, Britain and the US the annual rates of production and consumption are already far higher than are necessary, and much of our productive effort only churns out luxuries and wasteful items. We can only have our present high levels of consumption because the rich countries are taking most of the world's resource output. Even more important, there is no possibility of all the world's people rising to anything like the per capita levels of consumption and resource use that we have in rich countries at present. Despite all this the unquestionable goal is to keep our levels of production and consumption increasing all the time.

The present levels of output in the world are already causing serious resource and environmental problems; but if the rate of economic growth is 3 per cent, then by 2060 output will be *eight times* as high every year as it is now. To pursue such a goal must be to make all our global problems far worse, including resource scarcity, the deprivation of the Third World, tensions between nations, and especially the destruction of the environment. How many forests will be left and what will the greenhouse problem be like if we churn out eight times as many goods and services every year as we do now?

The limits to growth argument, detailed in Chapter 5, is that a peaceful, just and ecologically sustainable world order must be based on per capita levels of production and consumption that are *far lower* than our present levels. Yet we have an economy which must increase them all the time, and without end!

But why do we want growth?

At first it can sound plausible that if there is more output, more wealth is being produced, and there is more tax revenue for the government to spend on important projects — and therefore the better our living standards will be. However there are strong reasons for rejecting these assumptions.

◻ There is considerable evidence that the average quality of life is largely unrelated to change in the GNP. For example US GNP per capita more than doubled in a period of approximately 30 years after 1950 but various measures of the quality of life indicate that it did not rise, or that it fell. Many studies come to this general conclusion for rich countries.[1]

> '...once a person is above the poverty level, there is very little relationship between increased consumption and increased happiness.'
> D. Korten, *Sustainable Development*, (Duplicated MS) November, 1991, p.32.

◻ Are we better off just because we can buy more? A good quality of life depends on much more than the amount we can buy; it depends on such factors as the quality of the environment we live in, having satisfying work, being free from stress, having access to friends and a supportive community — all actually undermined when economic growth is the priority.

◻ Our concern should be to achieve *sufficient* living standards for comfort and convenience, not endlessly rising affluence. We should be trying to keep our level of consumption as low as possible, given that there is no possibility of all the world's people rising to the present rich country average level, and that this level is unsustainable because of the serious resource and environmental problems it is causing.

◻ It is often assumed that the more growth in the economy the more money the government will accumulate through taxes to spend on education, health, traffic problems, poverty and the environment etc. This is true but misleading. This 'trickle down' approach is extremely inefficient and at times totally ineffective. For every dollar it provides to the government to spend on the problems it devotes ten or more dollars to the production of things that suit people with capital to invest and people with disposable income to spend. Meanwhile the increased economic activity makes the problems worse – more traffic congestion, health problems and environmental damage. When we look back over recent decades it appears that the problems and the costs have outweighed the capacity of governments to deal with them despite the growth in tax income. The costs of health and other services have grown enormously. Most traffic, noise, pollution and other problems have become worse. Further, growth can hardly be claimed to be the means whereby poverty and inequality are to be reduced, given that despite considerable economic growth in the last decade poverty and inequality have increased even in rich countries.

In general better services are more likely to be achieved by revising goals and procedures, not by having more money to spend. For example changing from a curative to a preventative focus in medicine would probably make a large difference while enabling costs to fall.

¤ 'We need growth to solve the unemployment problem'. Again this seems plausible at first, but reflect on the fact that throughout the 1980s, when Australia achieved considerable economic growth, over 3 per cent p.a. on average, unemployment more or less doubled!

In our economy the increase in business activity and therefore employment will only be in those areas that maximise the return on invested capital. These are increasingly areas in which relatively little labour is employed. Over time there is development of more and more capital-intensive productive systems. Productivity, i.e, output per worker, increases at around 2 per cent p.a. in the long term, meaning that after each 35 years only half as many workers are needed to produce a given amount. In other words, when a government's economic priority is growth it is opting to increase those forms of business which will employ the *least* number of people per dollar of output. It would be quite possible to stimulate many other forms of activity which would give much more work to the many who want it, but this is completely ruled out on the grounds that it is costly and inefficient. Of course it would be more 'costly' and it would be associated with lower average 'living standards', but in

Chapter 12 it is argued that this is precisely what we must opt for in order to save the planet! The point is that we do not 'have to have growth to solve the unemployment problem' — there are other ways. It is the only conceivable way in *this* economy, where only strategies which facilitate the maximisation of output and profit are acceptable.

It is distressing that the absurdity of the unemployment problem is given so little attention. Because of our highly productive technology we really need *little employment.* In a sane economy we would be delighted to minimise the amount of dreary work, to do just that amount of work required to produce the things we need for a good living standard, sharing it between all workers, and to cut the average hours worked every time automation advanced. Yet here we are producing more than can easily be sold with officially around 6 to 10 per cent (in reality more like 15 per cent) of the workforce desperately crying for more jobs.

We have an unemployment problem because we have a capitalist economy; that is, because we have organised things in such a way that people cannot get work or incomes unless those in control of capital can make more money as a result of employing them. They will only employ more people if they can sell more products profitably, which is often quite difficult in an economy characterised by overproduction, recession and waste. ('Communist' economies can have an unemployment problem too, but the economy of an Israeli Kibbutz settlement doesn't.)

Contrast this with the domestic or household economy, where sanity does prevail. Within one's household the work needed is usually shared among the available workers and as soon as it's done all can relax, with no problem of unemployment. Similarly, any technical advance simply means increased leisure for all. There is no problem of unemployment in that economy because it is not run on capitalist lines.

The obsession with growth as the supreme goal in our society can be seen as one of the key elements in the dominant capitalist ideology. The things that would do most to improve the quality of life for most people on more or less average incomes are not very likely to result from increasing their incomes or the income of the nation. However, constantly increasing the amount of economic turnover is of the utmost importance to the few who own capital and to the technocrats, managers and financiers working for them. Unless more factories can be opened from year to year they will not be able to find profitable investments for their ever-accumulating volumes of capital.

The crucial assumption;
growth = development = progress

Conventional development economics is based on the mistaken and vicious assumption that to stimulate more economic turnover is to promote development. There is now a considerable critical literature making the following points.

◻ When stimulating as much growth in economic output as possible is the goal, the typical result is highly *inappropriate* development; that is, it is development of things other than those most likely to meet the most urgent needs of most people.

◻ Often the most appropriate development would occur if the available development resources were put into developments that reduced the GNP, such as into building village workshops, food storage and forest gardens(which would mean less food would be bought).

◻ Often the most appropriate development would be promoted if highly profitable developments such as setting up more export plantations were prevented.

◻ Progress should be seen in terms of a desirable state to which we are trying to move. We should be trying to develop local economic systems into a form or structure which we think will maximise the welfare, security and quality of life of all. This is a totally different business to simply encouraging the amount of economic turnover to increase constantly. It is argued in Chapter 12 that in a desirable economy most of the real economy would be outside the cash sector, many goods would be free and many would be produced by cooperative and voluntary work. At some stage our local economy would have been *sufficiently developed*. Conventional economists have no conception of reaching such a point in time, let alone of an economy becoming overdeveloped, because the only way they think of development is in terms of the economy constantly growing in its volume of production for sale.

… And trickle down?

The trickle down part of the formula is another crucial assumption in conventional economics. The claim is that when those with capital to invest set up factories and sell things, even though they might only be things richer people can afford, little people can get jobs in those factories and their take home pay will enable them to buy more of what they need, thereby creating a demand for more factories and jobs for other people. Similarly, when the new firms and income earners pay taxes, the government accumulates more money to spend on pensions and hospitals. Thus the idea is not to apply our society's productive capacity directly to producing the most urgently needed things, but to give the business sector the incentive and the freedom to 'create more wealth so there will be more to trickle down to all'.

The growth and trickle down philosophy is strongly opposed to solving problems such as poverty through greater redistribution of income from rich to poor. Hence the common claim: 'You have to create wealth before it can be redistributed'. But this overlooks the fact that we already have far more production and wealth than would be needed to give a high quality of life to all were they distributed at all sensibly, or if the right things were produced.

Conventional economists almost never use the term 'trickle down' but they do at times talk about the importance of 'baking a bigger cake', or claim that 'a rising tide lifts all boats'. Nevertheless 'trickle down' is obviously the crucial assumption underlying conventional economics. Its inadequacy is most glaring in the recent history of Third World development. The development literature has made clear for decades now that *very, very little ever trickles down*. Despite remarkable economic growth in the Third World little has been done to meet the needs of the poorest people and the numbers in extreme poverty have increased. During the 1980s the world as a whole became much richer but most Third World people probably became poorer; certainly many hundreds of millions of people did so, at a rate that cannot be explained fully by rapid population growth.

The failure of wealth to trickle down is also glaringly obvious within the richest countries. For example, between 1966 and 1976, Australian Gross National Product (GNP) increased by 61 per cent, from $113 billion to $182 billion. Despite this huge increase the poorest one-fifth of Australians increased their total incomes by only $2.4 billion in that period, while the richest one-fifth increased theirs by $41 billion. The poorest one-fifth actually ended up with a smaller share of GNP, 5.4 per cent in 1976 compared with 6.6 per cent in 1966, while the share of GNP going to the rich rose from 39 per cent to 47 per cent. In other words, despite a large increase in Australian wealth there was very little trickle down. Average per capita income rose by more than 25 per cent in the 10 years to 1988, yet by several accounts the real living standards of most working people in Australia and the US have fallen. (See Chapter 8.)

Fig. 4.1: How GDP Rises While Welfare Falls

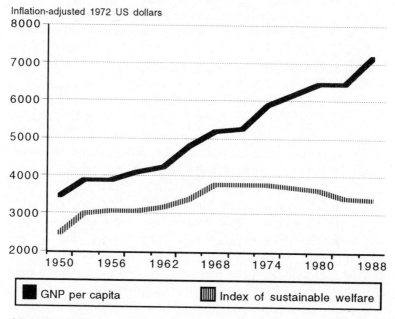

Inflation-adjusted 1972 US dollars

■ GNP per capita   ▥ Index of sustainable welfare

Adapted from H. Daly and J. Cobb, *For the Common Good*, London, Green Print, 1989, p420.

Consider the record!

Those who persist in advocating the growth and trickle down approach seem to have no understanding of how very badly it has performed, even in relation to conventional criteria such as unemployment and debt. Australian 'living standards' defined in terms of GNP per capita (in constant dollars) have increased enormously since the 1950s, multiplying about 2.5 times. Surely a society experiencing such a vast increase in wealth could have solved all its problems of poverty, inadequate hospitals and environmental damage long ago. *But look at the record.* In about one decade to 1990 unemployment doubled, one measure of poverty almost doubled, the farm debt multiplied by 9, and the foreign debt multiplied by 10!! In addition, national independence, the situation with regard to foreign ownership, and especially ecological conditions, all deteriorated alarmingly. Chapter 8 adds the fact that many measures of the quality of life and social breakdown also showed disturbing trends.

The system simply does not deliver. And from here on it will provide less well for a diminishing number of people — see Chapter 10.

Yet we are supposed to accept that making the growth of business turnover the top priority is without question the most effective way to improve 'living standards' — and just about all politicians, journalists and economists do believe this! Some natural phenomena defy comprehension.

In the US, real wages have fallen since 1972 and official statistics show an increase in the number of people unemployed and living in poverty.[2] Yet real GDP per capita *doubled* between 1950 and 1990. Daly and Cobb have developed an Index of Sustainable Economic Welfare taking into account 20 factors including many costs and environmental conditions, such as soil loss. Figure 4.1 shows that while US GNP has risen this index has fallen for twenty years.

Experience seems to show that, except in extraordinary boom times such as between 1950 and 1970, making the supreme economic goal 'the baking of a bigger cake' will do little or nothing to raise the real living standards of most people. In fact the evidence from the Third World seems to show clearly that in general *growth impoverishes!* It certainly enriches some, but when the main development goal is to increase business turnover as much as possible, the poorest perhaps 50 per cent in a Third World country will tend to be deprived of the productive capacity they once had. (See Chapter 7.)

Chapter 5 argues that not only has the mindless pursuit of growth ceased delivering benefits to most of us, but it is now the direct cause of our most serious global problems.

The wastefulness and inefficiency of the trickle down approach

Let's assume that significant trickle down was occurring. Even so, a 'growth and trickle down' strategy is quite *indiscriminate*. There is no concern with what things are produced or whether they are worthwhile, or with ensuring that the most appropriate and needed things are produced first. The goal is just to encourage more and more production of anything at all. The result tends to be more luxury items, since the people with most money to spend are more likely to buy these. The idea is that the more production of anything the better because then there will be more jobs, income for people and tax revenue for the government. But we do not need any more luxury goods and we desperately do need more cheap housing and good hospitals! Clearly this is an extremely wasteful and inefficient way to proceed.

> 'President Eisenhower's advice to the American nation during a
> period of economic downturn... "Buy anything." '
> D.E. Shi, *The Simple Life*, New York, Oxford University Press, 1985, p250.

Consider what happens when a dollar is invested in frivolous or luxurious production. About 20c-30c would be paid to workers for that amount of output, yielding perhaps 6c-8c in taxes. The company might make 10c profit and pay about 3c in company tax. So the government would receive about 10c in tax. Only a small proportion of this would then be available for spending on vitally needed things like housing or welfare for people, maybe one-thirtieth of the amount that would have been available had the whole dollar been put into building cheap housing!

Now consider the wastefulness and inefficiency of the system from another angle. The first graph in Fig 4.2 shows the approximate wage and salary distribution in Australia. (Additional income in other forms such as capital gains, is not shown here; most of it also goes to the richest few). Little more of the income of higher income people would need to be transferred to the poorest people to lift them all above the poverty line. In fact, only about another 4 per cent of all income would be sufficient to do this. But the conventional view is strongly opposed to any more redistribution; it insists that the best solution is to 'bake a bigger cake'.

The second graph represents a doubling of all the incomes in the first graph and therefore a cake of national wealth twice as big. Now, most of the increased wealth could only be spent on luxuries because even in the previous case about half of the people had more than adequate incomes. So instead of transferring 4 per cent of national income in order to lift everyone out of poverty, the growth strategy would greatly increase the national income and consumption, and the amount spent on luxuries! There could hardly be a more wasteful and inefficient solution if the aim were to solve social problems. And what a delightful strategy for the already rich; let's solve problems like poverty and hospitals by a method that delivers $10 or $20 to us for every $1 it delivers to the government to spend on those problems.

Remember the most important point to be made about this general trickle down strategy is not how inefficient it is when it works, but that often it does not work at all, and indeed the reverse effect can occur. Again, in rich countries a much bigger cake was being baked at the end of the 1980s but many problems including unemployment,

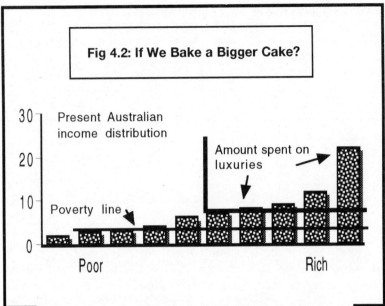

Fig 4.2: If We Bake a Bigger Cake?

If present incomes were doubled to lift everyone above the poverty line, there would be a huge increase in the consumption of luxuries:

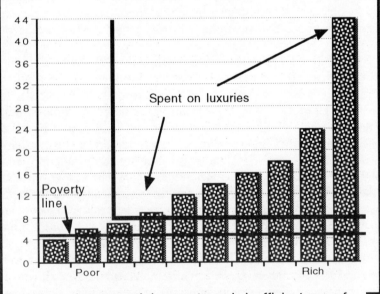

Hence sheer growth is an extremely inefficient way of satisfying the most urgent needs

poverty and debt had become much worse.

The basic fault revealed by the trickle down philosophy is that we do not have an economy in which the members of a society somehow work out what they want produced and then produce and distribute it according to need and other agreed criteria. Instead, we have an economy in which what is produced is determined by what will make most money for those few with capital. Everyone else is supposed to be content with the products and jobs and trickle down benefits this process delivers to us. The system functions primarily for the benefit of those with capital. Of course they can't maximise their incomes unless they attend to what we want, but they can and do maximise it without attending to what should be produced to maximise many factors such as justice, welfare, the quality of life for all, and ecological sustainability. How absurd that we let a very few rich people control, indeed own, most of 'our' economy and operate it for their benefit, yet we remain content with whatever benefits this yields us! In a sane society we would have mechanisms whereby we all participated in the ownership and control of the systems for producing, distributing and exchanging things and we would operate them to provide directly for all, rather than rely on the indirect consequences of processes run primarily for the benefit of those with capital.

The quality of life

The most basic question to ask of any social system or practice is whether or not it increases the experienced quality of life. After all, there would be no sense in increasing our incomes or the number of supermarkets if these changes did not make us enjoy life any more than we used to. There is much evidence that economic growth is not increasing our experienced quality of life. Many surveys have found that in a rich country there is no relation between increases in income and the quality of life. Even over periods of decades when real incomes have doubled, the rates at which people say they are happy or measure their wellbeing typically do not increase.[1] Douthwaite's *The Growth Illusion* (1991) is a large and heavily documented recent book arguing in detail that economic growth is simply not improving our lives.

Chapter 8 goes further and explains that when we make growth of the economy our goal we actually facilitate the breakdown of society, the disruption of community, the destruction of towns, and the generation of an impoverished, alienated and dangerous underclass. Just consider what is happening in the rich countries in general now. Despite considerable economic growth over the last decade it is obvious that on many dimensions our society has deteriorated. Most social problems have become more serious, especially those to do with people condemned to unemployment. Country towns and rural life are gradually dying. Urban life is becoming more congested and polluted. Drug problems and violence are increasing. There is more concern about security, especially from theft and violence. Increasing numbers are homeless, alcoholic or suffering mental breakdown. Chapter 8 will explain that when getting the economy going is seen as the most important goal, many things are done which intensify these effects, such as reducing the need for paid labour and reducing investment in less profitable regions. Often the most desirable or appropriate thing to do is not that which will most increase economic output.

It is most depressing that the public discussion of growth gives almost no attention to this crucial question, 'Is it making us any happier?' since the answer appears to be clearly, 'No!' We can buy more as the years go by (although even this is not true now for the average American) but surely that is not important if we do not enjoy life more. If we focused our social policy on measures of the experienced quality of life we would realise that it is most likely to be maximised with only a limited amount of production for sale and with many economic needs met outside the market and the cash sector, and that there are many areas of society that are far more important for the quality of life than the economy.

Growth and war

If all nations continue to strive for increased living standards and economic growth while resources become more and more scarce, there can be no other outcome than increasing struggles between nations for resources and markets.

As already stated, at 3 per cent p.a. growth our annual volume of production would be 8 times as great by 2060. Even with optimistic assumptions about energy and resource conservation the total demand for resources must increase markedly. The rich nations are far from self-sufficient in resource supply now and their imports from the Third World are increasing. The Third World is discontented about the rich countries taking most of the available resources. By 2060 their populations will probably outnumber ours by 6 or 8 to 1. Yet we all remain obsessed with achieving the fastest possible increases in production, consumption and GNP. Given these conditions it is difficult to imagine how we could possibly avoid more and more conflict between rich and poor nations over access to resources and markets in coming decades.

Joseph Schumpeter and others have argued that the nature of capitalism is opposed to imperialism and war.[4] Capitalism is said to work best and prosper most when there is free trade rather than the restricted markets colonialism establishes, and when there is greater freedom from disruption caused by war. These claims are quite acceptable but leave out the important part of the story. Many radical economists have pointed out that despite what capitalists might like, capitalism does inevitably lead towards imperialism and war in the long run. Imperialism and war might not result, but only if action to head them off is taken against the tendencies capitalism generates.

The basic factor here is that capitalism inescapably involves expansion. Capitalists only invest if they can make more money than they invest. They typically expect to make at least 10 per cent profit p.a. Some of this must go into repairing old plant, but there is a constant increase in the amount of money available for investment. In fact, capitalism's greatest long-term problem is to find enough profitable areas for investing the constantly accumulating volumes of capital. It is a system in which this problem regularly gives rise to slumps and recessions. For long periods this problem might be solved without generating armed conflicts, but from time to time it does lead *towards* war because capitalists looking for new ventures tend to get in each others' way. They find themselves competing with businesses from other countries for access to resources and markets, and they are always ready to call upon their governments to help them protect against or overcome the competition.

This is not to say that *only* economic factors cause international conflict, but there is an extensive literature on the central role of economic factors, especially where a rising power threatens to overtake the dominant one.

A glance at modern history shows that there has always been a struggle between the biggest states to grab most of the wealth and prestige and power and to disadvantage others. The main source of conflict and war in the world is the ceaseless quest for greater wealth and power. *We have no chance of achieving a peaceful world until nations stop being greedy and work out how to live without constantly striving to grow richer.* Yet the supreme commitment in our economy is to rapid and ceaseless growth!

'...expansion is a prime source of conflict. So long as the dynamics of differential growth remain unmanaged, it is probable that these long-term processes will sooner or later carry major powers into war.

'War is mainly explicable in terms of differential growth in a world of scarce and unevenly distributed resources...'
R. Ashley, *The Political Economy of War and Peace*, 1980, pp3,126.

'War is an inevitable result of the struggle between economies for expansion.'
R.A. Nettleship, *War: Its Causes and Correlates*, The Hague, Mouton, 1975, p497.

Choucri and North say their most important finding is that domestic growth is a strong determinant of national expansion and that this results in competition between nations and war.
See N. Choucri and R.S. North, *Nations in Conflict*, San Francisco, Freeman, 1975, p278.

'...warfare appears as a normal and periodic form of competition within the capitalist world economy.'
'...world wars regularly occur during a period of economic expansion.'
Statements referred to by C. Chase-Dunn, *Global Formation*, 1989, pp108, 163.

It is possible that for a long time to come the transnational corporations from the rich countries can go on securing most of the world's resources and markets without clashing and drawing their governments into armed conflict. But the tendency for this to happen must increase as resources and markets become more scarce. The only satisfactory way to remove this dangerous tendency is by shifting to an economic system which permits us to live comfortably without constantly striving for economic growth.

We must understand that the problem of world peace is part of the problem of global economic justice. So long as we refuse to bring about a fairer distribution of the world's wealth, which means de-development on the part of the rich and over-developed countries, we can only expect continued and accelerating conflict and violence.

> 'Struggles are taking place, or are in the offing, between rich and poor nations over their share of the world product, within the industrial world over their share of industrial resources and markets...'
> D. Barnet, 'Multinationals in Third World Development', in *Multinational Monitor*, 1980, p29.
>
> 'Finite resources in a world of expanding populations and increasing per capita demands create a situation ripe for international violence.'
> P. Ehrlich, A. Ehrlich and J. Holdren, *Ecoscience*, San Francisco, Freeman, 1977, p60.

The limits to growth

The main point being argued in this chapter is that the growth and trickle-down strategy does not work at all satisfactorily. Chapter 5 will add the argument that even if it were now raising poorer people towards satisfactory living standards at a reasonable rate, it could not in future succeed in this goal because of resource and environmental limits. There is no chance of all people ever rising to the living standards people in rich countries have now. Yet conventional development theory never questions this goal.

NOTES

1 H. Daly & J. Cobb, *For the Common Good*, London, Green Print, 1989, p453. R. Easterlin, 'Does money buy happiness?' in R.C. Puth (ed), *Current Issues in the American Economy*, Lexington, Heath 1976. R. Douthwaite, *The Growth Illusion*, Hartland, Green Books, 1992.
2 Daly and Cobb, *op. cit.*, p.410. D. Dowd, *The Waste of Nations*, Boulder, Westview, 1989.
3 *U.S. Statistical Abstract*, 1991.
4 J. Schumpeter, *Imperialism and Social Classes*, New York, Meridian, 1955, pp55, 89.

5

The limits to growth

THE 'LIMITS TO GROWTH' movement which has developed over the last three decades is based on the argument that the way of life in rich countries is unsustainable, primarily because it involves huge resource and environmental costs. The pursuit of more affluent living standards and more economic growth is now the major cause of several serious global problems, including environmental destruction, Third World deprivation, conflict, and resource scarcity. The solution must be to shift eventually to a zero-growth economy on much lower resource use and GNP per capita than we have in the few overdeveloped countries.

This view clashes head on with conventional economic thinking, which is entirely built on the assumption that endless economic growth is without question possible, desirable and very important. There is no concept of any limits or point at which there has been sufficient development, nor is there any concept of *over*development. It is simply assumed that economic output can and should go on increasing as fast as possible for ever.

Here are the main themes in the limits to growth view of our global situation.

Resource limits

Our way of life is extremely expensive in terms of resources, energy and the environment. We are obliged to use up huge quantities of non-renewable resources. US energy consumption averages the equivalent of 12 tonnes of coal per person per year, 6 times the world average and 30 times the average for the poorest half of the world's people.

Some of the most persuasive limits to growth arguments concern the huge amount of travel and transport that take place in our present society. Goods are shipped around the world, people travel to work and go long distances for holidays, and food is transported a long way to where it is consumed. The average amount of road transport per person in Australia is more than 9000 km every year. There is no realistic possibility of keeping up anything like this amount of transport when oil runs short as is most likely in a few decades time.

Economists often give the misleading impression that resource availability depends mainly on the price we are prepared to pay, so that resource scarcity can be overcome if price and demand rise. In the short term there is a tendency for this to happen, but the important limits to the availability of resources are biological and geological. Changes in the price of oil, for instance, make no difference to the amount that exists in recoverable form within the ground. Approximately fifty estimates have been made of the total amount of potentially recoverable oil deposits and the median of these is around 2000 billion barrels. This would only last about 10 years if everyone in the world today used it at the US per capita average.

Only a very small proportion of the minerals existing in the earth's crust has been concentrated into ore deposits, probably less than 0.1 per cent, and the rest exist thinly, and mostly in the form of silicates. To extract a kg of metal from its richest occurrence in silicates would take 10 to 100 times as much energy as to extract it from the poorest ore deposit. This cost will be prohibitive given our energy situation.[1] Estimates of the potentially recoverable mineral and energy resources available in ore deposits have become available since the early 1970s. These cannot be taken as very reliable but they provide a useful reference point for thinking about how sustainable our resource-expensive way of life might be. If we assume 10 per cent of the ore deposits (a) will be found, (b) will have ore rich enough to mine, (c) will be big enough to warrant building a mine, and (d) are accessible for mining, most of the mineral resource items would be exhausted quickly if all the people likely to be on earth after 2050 (11 billion) were to use them at the present rich world per capita rate.[2] Of the basic 28 minerals, 12 would be exhausted in under 40 years, including copper, tin, lead, gold, mercury, silver and zinc.

These conclusions refer to all deposits in the crust to a depth of 4.6 km. The geological processes that form mineral deposits tend to occur mostly within the top few kilometres of the crust. In addition the difficulty of finding and mining deposits increase with depth, due to heat and faults in the rocks, for example. Thus in practice it is not likely that much mining will be carried out at greater than 2 km depth. Indeed if the most plausible assumptions are made regarding the above factors limiting the proportion of deposits likely to be accessible, only around 2 per cent of them — rather than 10 per cent — would be retrieved. Eighteen items would then be exhausted in less than 30 years.

In the one hundred years to 1970, costs of minerals continually fell. Whether that trend has ceased now is debated.[3] However, trends in dollar costs can be quite misleading indicators of real scarcity. For example the price of oil has fallen since the early 1980s, but oil is in fact becoming more scarce, and there will probably be little left by 2040. Similarly, present trends in the price of rainforest timber give no indication that by 2040 there will probably be none of that left either.

Much more important than the dollar costs per unit of mineral produced are the energy costs, and the capital costs. These have been increasing for some time and are likely to accelerate. The long-term energy cost of producing minerals and energy has been rising at 2–3 per cent p.a. and is likely to go on doing so.[4] At this rate the energy cost of a tonne will double every 30 years or so, indicating that technical advance is not making these items more abundantly available as time goes by.

Services?

It is sometimes assumed that resource scarcity will not hinder economic growth because from here on the growth will mostly take place in the service sector. However, services use surprising quantities of materials and energy, for offices, lighting etc. Some of the biggest service industries are transport, tourism and travel; very energy intensive activities. Many service industries deal with material goods, such as insurance, advertising, transport, and retailing. Even if they used no material resources once they are established, growth in the number of service firms in existence would involve growth in the resources required for construction and equipment. Let us assume that from here on economic growth of 3 per cent p.a. takes place but it is all within the service sector. By 2060 the service sector would make up 96 per cent of the total economy and would be 12 times as big as it is now! It is not plausible that an economy churning out 8 times as much as at present would not have a much greater resource throughput than now.

It is sometimes argued that we could continue to pursue economic growth if we changed to a sensible definition of it; in other words, if we defined the GNP or overall economic welfare in a way that reliably reflected real economic costs and benefits. Such an index might subtract expenditure that had to be devoted to cleaning up pollution, and it might take into account the real benefits associated with improving the friendliness, security and cultural tone of our living places. Could we not constantly and ceaselessly increase the 'production and consumption' of knowledge, courses, personal development, conviviality and satisfying life experience?

We obviously do need more sensible measures of overall economic wealth or welfare, but none of this can change the crucial fact about our present economic system. It must have constant and limitless growth in GNP *as this is now defined,* i.e. production for sale. Unless dollar and pound turnover and returns on investment increase all the time and create more and more profitable investment outlets for all that ever-accumulating capital there is serious trouble in this economy.

Energy limits

The resource limits seem to be even clearer with respect to energy. The most common estimates of the potentially recoverable energy resources seem to be (in tonnes of coal equivalent): coal 1000 billion, oil 315 billion, gas 500 billion, shale oil 200 billion, uranium 160 billion.[5] Even if we double the coal figure, and if all the people the world is likely to have in 2060 were to use energy at the per capita rate people in rich countries average today, this total volume of energy would be completely exhausted in a mere 20 years.

Those who wish to argue that the energy problem can be solved by nuclear energy should realise that 250,000 giant reactors would be needed, 1000 times the world's present nuclear capacity. They would have to be breeder reactors until fusion became viable (and it might not be viable), meaning 1 million tonnes of plutonium in constant use!

Nor should it be assumed that all we have to do is simply change from fossil fuels to renewable energy sources like the sun and the wind. These are sources we will all live well on one day, but we will almost certainly do so only at very frugal levels of energy use, because they are very difficult and costly to collect and store.

The biggest problems for renewable energy sources concern the provision of electricity and liquid fuels. Impressive figures for solar and wind energy are often cited, but these refer to the best experimental sites and do not take into account the very high storage and transport costs and losses that would be associated with attempting to base current rich world living standards on renewable energy sources. Most rich world people live in high latitudes. If Europe's winter electricity demand were to be supplied by solar plants located in Northern Africa and pumping hydrogen to Europe, then approximately 95 per cent of the energy collected would be lost in conversion, storage, or transmission. (For a detailed explanation, see *The Conserver Society*, Chapter 9.) At present-day photovoltaic cell efficiencies (13 per cent in the field) and costs (A\$500/m² wholesale), the cost of the 200 million m² of cells for a power system supplying 1000 MW in Europe would be A\$100 billion. This is 40 times the cost of a coal fired plant plus coal for 20 years. (At 20% efficiency and A\$200/m², optimistic but possible future figures, the cost of the cells would be \$22.2 billion, around 10 times the cost of a coal fired power station.) Note that these figures do not take into account the cost of operation, maintenance, insurance, profits and interest payments on the capital that would have to be borrowed. These items might double the above cost for the cells. Industrialised economies could not survive anything like this multiple of the present cost of electricity.

It also appears that rich countries, especially Australia and many in Europe, will be unlikely to derive more than a small proportion of their electricity from the wind, both because of the lack of sites with good wind that have not been taken for other purposes, and the unreliability of the winds. There is always a chance that most of the mills will not be turning at a given time, so there is always a need for many power stations of other types. It is generally agreed that this factor will limit windmills to contributing only 5–20 per cent of the electricity generated by a system, unless it can be stored. Nor is there enough land to fuel the present world car fleet on liquid fuels produced from plant matter.[6] (If 10 billion people had American levels of car ownership, the fleet would be more than 10 times as big.)

While technical advances are likely to reduce the costs associated with renewables considerably, the magnitude of the reductions required would seem to be quite impossible to attain.[7] It should be stressed that these arguments concern the improbability of meeting *present levels* of energy demand from renewable sources, yet if the expected 11 billion people are to live as rich people do today then *10 times* present world energy production will be required, and if they all have 3 per cent economic growth the energy will have to be found to double output every 23 years thereafter.

Energy conservation and pollution control?

Energy conservation measures are also unlikely to alter this picture significantly. At present considerable savings are being made as attention is given to introducing more energy-efficient technologies. This will probably continue for many years, given that our history of energy extravagance has left much fat to trim. The most common estimates seem to indicate that rich countries might eventually be able to cut their present per capita energy use by half.[8] If 10 billion people were to rise to that total level world energy production would have to be about 5 times as great as it is today — which, as the previous discussion indicates, it is far beyond the capacity of renewables to meet.

The same logic applies to better pollution control. If we cut by 33 per cent the environmental impact caused per dollar of GNP but keep economic output increasing at 3 per cent p.a., then in only 14 years total impact will be as high as it was before the cut, and in another 23 years it will be twice as high.

The most important point here is that *if there remains any commitment to growth in economic output, any plausible cuts in energy use will be overwhelmed in time* by the increase in energy needed to produce the increasing volumes of output. For example, if we were to have 3 per cent economic growth until 2060, i.e. eight times more production in 2060 than now, the energy use or environmental impact per unit of output would have to be one-eighth of what it is now just to keep the total energy use or impact from rising above present levels.

Resource conclusions

This examination of the scarcity of resources leads to the crucial 'limits to growth' conclusion. *It is not possible for all the world's people to rise to the rates of per capita resource and energy use enjoyed by the one-fifth of the world's people who live in rich countries today.*

This means that we are the *overdeveloped* countries and the rest are the *never-to-be-developed* countries. We can only be as affluent as we are because we are hogging most of the dwindling resources. If we are to remain as affluent as we are, the rest must remain much poorer than we are.

While the rich countries take more than three-quarters of the resources produced in the world, most people are deprived of basic necessities. Many of the resources we consume in rich countries are exported from poor countries, including large quantities of food. At least 40,000 people die every day because of deprivation. Our resource expensive way of life is therefore not just impossible to sustain, it is morally indefensible.

Our way of life is ecologically unsustainable

Our resource-affluent way of life also causes many serious environmental problems. We are destroying vital ecological systems. Consider, for example, the greenhouse problem, acid rain, the destruction of forests, the spread of deserts and the loss of plant and animal species. At the present rate, more than a million species will disappear in the next 25 years, because the expansion of human economic activity is destroying habitats. We farm in ways that lose 5 tonnes of topsoil for each person on earth every year (that is 15 times the amount of food we eat), we are destroying the protective ozone layer in the atmosphere, and we are polluting the ground waters and seas.

One of the most unsustainable aspects of our society is the way we continually take large quantities of nutrients from the soil, eat them and then throw them away. We are depleting our soils at a rapid rate. In Chapter 12 it will be argued that we can only have a sustainable agriculture if we change to highly localised economic systems in which most of our food is produced close to where we live and all food wastes can be recycled.

> '...the environmental crisis... is the inevitable consequence of exponential growth in a finite environment.'
> R. Turner, *A Short Course in Economics*, 1991

Most of these ecological problems are direct consequences of the sheer amount of producing and consuming going on. There is, for example, no way of solving the greenhouse problem without drastically reducing the amount of fuel being burnt, and therefore the volume of production taking place. The Intergovernmental Panel on Climate Change has concluded that in order to keep the carbon content of the atmosphere from increasing, let alone reduce it (as we should be doing) we will have to cut carbon input to the atmosphere by 60–80 per cent. If by 2060 we achieve a 60 per cent reduction and share the energy among 11 billion people then world average fossil fuel use would be about one-eighteenth the present Australian average. How can we do anything like this unless we drastically reduce energy use and therefore fossil fuel use?

One of the most disturbing recent observations is the fact that in the last decade a number of crucial biological and ecological indices seem to be approaching or to have passed their peaks. This is true of world cropland area, irrigated area, fertiliser use, and meat, timber, wool and grain production. Some key yields such as rice and wheat seem to be tapering towards upper limits. World fish catch has clearly fallen from levels that will not be attained again. Yet we are only providing well for one billion people, and we might soon have 11 billion on the planet.

Now add to this analysis the implications of continued economic growth. Fig 6.1a represents the present volume of world economic output, distributed across its 5.4 billion people. Figure 6.1b represents output assuming that all the people living in the Third World in 2060 have risen to the living standards the rich countries have now, and incomes in rich countries rise by 3 per cent p.a. until then. World output would be about 19 times as great as it is now. Anyone assuming that all the world's people can be as rich as the rich world's people would be by 2060, given only 3 per cent annual growth until then, must believe that the world's resources and ecosystems can sustain *88 times present annual volumes of output*. And 3 per cent growth rate is not sufficient to make our economy healthy! In the 1980s Australia averaged 3.2 per cent annual growth and just about all its economic and social problems became worse. Unemployment at least doubled and the foreign debt multiplied by 10. Prime Minister Keating has emphasised that we need 4.5 per cent growth to start bringing unemployment down. Let us assume we were to average 4 per cent annual growth until 2060, and that by then all the world's people had risen to the 'living standards' we would have then. Total world economic output would be *220 times* what it is today.

There is no chance whatsoever of reaching even a 19-fold increase in present output. Yet conventional economists proceed as if we can rise to and beyond these levels; they never acknowledge any need to worry about there being any limits to the growth of production and consumption.

The environmental problem is basically due to overproduction and overconsumption, yet we have an economy in which there must be constant and limitless increase in production and consumption. Again, the problem is due to our economy and cannot be solved until we develop a quite different economy.

'But the market will solve resource scarcities'

Economists usually believe that we need not worry about resource scarcity because as supplies dwindle prices will rise, giving the incentive for more to be discovered, or for poorer ores to be processed, or for substitutes to be used. It is true that over some periods of time these mechanisms actually increased the quantities of resources available for use, despite the fact that increasing quantities were being used up.

But this argument fails to recognise that there are limits to these mechanisms which are set by the biophysical nature of the planet. There is a finite amount of oil in the ground, in various forms; of zinc in ore deposits of differing grades; and of farm land of differing quality. Yes: as some of these categories are exhausted it is possible to move on to exploit more difficult categories, but don't conclude that economics is creating resources that were not there before. What is happening is that more of the finite options are being used up. Yes: when conventional oil has gone, price increases might make it attractive to start using shale oil — but that is limited too.

It is probable that technical advances will generate new options in some fields for a long time yet. Bet overall such options are clearly running out, most seriously in biological and ecological realms. Is it plausible that given the present intense level of scarcity, price rises plus technical advance can sustain 8 or 16 times as much output seventy years from now, and double that level every twenty years thereafter?

The Third World problem

As will be detailed in Chapter 7, an economy based on the pursuit of affluence and growth is the prime cause of poverty, hunger and underdevelopment in the Third World. At first this might seem paradoxical because the conventional view is that growth in the rich countries increases opportunities for the Third World to prosper by exporting things to us, and that growth in the Third World will yield trickle down benefits to all Third World people.

This economy produces extremely unequal distributions of the world's resources. Most resources are being consumed by the few of the world's people who live in rich countries. They make up only 20 per cent of the world's population but they are consuming 75 per cent of the output of resources. Their per capita rate of consumption of energy is around 17 times that of the poorest half of the world's people.

In other words resources are really extremely scarce already; most of the world's people have almost no access to most of them. If world resource output were to be shared more or less equally, each person in the rich countries would receive only about one quarter of the amount we get now. Then we would recognise a problem of scarcity! Similarly, if all the world's people were to use as many resources per capita as we in rich countries do, the total rate of resource use would jump and in a few decades we would have completely exhausted about half the minerals and all the energy.

The second important criticism of the economy in this context is that the growth and trickle down approach to development does little more than enrich the rich. Clearly it is not solving the problems experienced by most Third World people at a tolerable rate, if at all. When 'getting the economy going' and increasing business turnover is the goal of development, the things developed are not those that will serve the urgent needs of most people. The result is development of the industries that meet the demand of the urban rich and the consumers in the rich countries. Hence, what we have had is inappropriate development; development in the interests of the rich. The Third World has developed plantations and mines which are the means whereby most Third World land, capital and labour have become geared to the interests of the transnational corporations and the consumers in the rich countries, with negligible benefit to most Third World people.

In any case — and as has been explained above — it is not possible for the poor countries to rise to rich world living standards. This does not mean that Third World economies should not grow. It means that *if getting them to grow is the main goal, the wrong things will be developed*. The goal should be to develop the things that are most needed, and then any consequent growth in the economy would be seen as a relatively incidental outcome.

Much literature now argues that the global economy is extremely unjust and that satisfactory development for the Third World will not be possible unless the rich countries stop taking so much of the world's wealth, permit the Third World's labour, land and capital to be invested in the production of necessities, and cease supporting greedy and repressive Third World regimes eager to keep their countries to policies that benefit us. This view is aptly summarised by the saying, 'The rich must live more simply so that the poor may simply live.' Both rich and poor nations should change to a development model which provides modest but satisfactory living standards through largely self-sufficient local settlements. The growth and trickle down approach to development is the cause of the most serious Third World problems, not their solution.

Conflict

In Chapter 4 it was pointed out that our mindless obsession with endlessly raising living standards and GNP is generating many forms of conflict in the world. If all countries insist on striving for higher and higher levels of production and consumption, in a world where resources are becoming scarce and population will double, then the only possible outcome must be more and more fierce struggles for access to dwindling resources and markets.

Quality of life

Chapter 4 also argued that the pursuit of growth does not improve quality of life. Many people would agree that the quality of life in the richest countries is falling now. Most social problems have become more serious in the last 20 years. When increasing production for sale is the supreme goal, governments are most concerned to do what will help firms prosper, and this means resources tend not to be made available for the development of cohesive and supportive communities, or to assist the most disadvantaged groups, or to solve environmental problems that reduce the quality of life. Even more important is the way that emphasis on increasing output and the scope for market forces undermines the non-material values that are crucial for a good society, especially the readiness of people to give, to cooperate and to help each other.

Is there any alternative?

These many and serious global problems are not separate. They are all consequences of the one basic mistake, the commitment to affluence and growth. They are all being generated by the pursuit of material living standards which it is not possible for all to have, and by the determination of even the richest societies to raise their living standards as far and as fast as possible.

Since the mid-1970s a considerable movement for radical change in economic thinking and practice has developed. A number of writers, groups and institutions are now arguing that global problems cannot be solved unless we move to an economy in which we can just produce as little as we need for good material lifestyles, with as little resource use and environmental impact as possible, and without any concern to increase levels of consumption over time. Chapter 12 will argue that it would not be at all difficult to develop such an economy, if sufficient numbers of people wanted to do so.

It is extremely important that the issue of limits to growth is placed centrally on the agenda of public debate, in the media, in schools and in parliaments. The possibility and desirability of growth and affluence are hardly ever doubted, and vast teams of bureaucrats, politicians, business and union leaders, journalists, and teachers as well as economists are continually working hard to promote growth and raise 'living standards'. They fail to see that these goals are now the source of our most serious global problems.

NOTES

1 J.E. Tilton and B.J. Skinner, 'The meaning of resources', in B.J. Skinner and D.J. McLaren (eds.), *Resources and World Development*, New York, Wiley, 1987, p22.

2 F.E. Trainer, 'How long will resources last?' (In press.) This discussion is based on figures given by B.J. Skinner, 1987, 'Supplies of geochemically scarce metals', in B.J. Skinner and P.C. McClaren, (eds), *Resources and World Development*, New York, Wiley, p316.

3 D.C. Hall and J. V. Hall, 'Concepts and measures of natural resource scarcity with a summary of recent trends', in *Journal of Environmental and Economic Management*, 11, 1984, p363. H. Daly and J. Cobb, *For the Common Good*, London, Green Print, 1989, p406.

4 P. Chapman and F. Roberts, *Metal Resources and Energy*, London, Butterworths, 1983.

5 F.E. Trainer, *Abandon Affluence!*, London, Zed Books, 1985, Chapter 4.

6 D. Pimentel et al., 'Renewable energy', in *Bioscience*, (in press, 1994). F.E. Trainer, *The Conserver Society*, London, Zed Books, 1995, Chapter 9.

7 For very optimistic claims concerning the potential of renewables see T.B. Johansson et al. (eds.), *Renewable Energy*, Washington, Island Press, 1993. These conclusions are based on questionable assumptions, eg. a sustainable world average forest biomass yield of 15 tonnes per ha, when even 3 tonnes is problematic given the need to recycle nutrients to the soil; see Pimentel, note 6 above.

8 General estimates are quoted in F.E. Trainer, *The Conserver Society*, London, Zed Books, 1995, Chapter 9.

6

Inequality

THE LAST TWO chapters discussed the general concept of trickle down as the mechanism for providing for people at the bottom of the heap. This chapter deals in more detail with the extent of inequality and with trends. Here and in Chapter 11, I argue that our present economy has a powerful tendency to generate greater inequality over time and we cannot expect to move towards reasonable levels of equity and social justice unless we change to a quite different economic system.

Inequality in income

Although Australia is better than most countries with respect to equality, there are very big differences in income and wealth. In 1990 the annual average income for the top 20 per cent of Australian income earners was $67,704, but for the bottom 20 per cent it was only $6,968.[1]

In the 1980s income distributions in rich countries including Australia generally became much more unequal and poverty increased.[2] Between 1981-82 and 1985-86 the proportion of national income going to the poorest one-fifth of Australians fell from 9.1 per cent to 8.5 per cent, while that going to the richest one-fifth rose 1.5 per cent to 35.8 per cent.[3] The real income of the poorest 10 per cent of British people fell by 9.7 per cent between 1979 and 1985 while the incomes of the top 20 per cent rose 22 per cent.[4] The richest 200 Australians increased their wealth from A$15 billion to A$20 billion in just one year. But the real incomes of most wage and salary earners have been falling for at least a decade.

Poverty

The most common measure of poverty in Australia, originally used by Professor Henderson, sets an austere poverty line; that is, if your income is under this line you are really struggling to get by. In the early 1970s about 8 per cent of Australians lived under the Henderson poverty line, another 10 per cent not far above it. The numbers appear to have increased significantly since then. The measure of income left after housing costs have been met, indicates an approximate doubling of the number of people living in poverty over the 10 years to 1985, when probably one-fifth of Australian children were living in poverty (double the 1972 proportion).[5] According to one source, the number of Australians living under the poverty line rose by 50 per cent between 1973 and 1987.[6] Elliott concludes that the proportion of Australian 'income units' in poverty rose from 10.7 per cent in 1981-2 to 16.7 per cent in 1989-90.[7] The number of Americans living in poverty rose from 26.1 million in 1979 to 34.4 million in 1987.[8]

Wealth and capital

The distribution of wealth is far more unequal than the distribution of income. The top 1 per cent of Australians own over 22 per cent of all wealth, as much as the bottom 70 per cent of people. The top 5 per cent have around 45 per cent of all wealth. In the USA the top 1 per cent probably own one-third of all wealth. There is little clear evidence on the distribution of ownership of capital but it is probably much more uneven than the wealth distribution. Ordinary people own a considerable proportion of national wealth in the form of houses, but many of these people have few, if any, net savings. While some institutions, such as pension funds, are considerable share 'owners', they represent large numbers of very small 'capitalists'. According to one estimate about half all income from investment goes to a mere 1 per cent of Australians, and 92 per cent goes to only 10 per cent.[9] In the USA, a mere 0.5 per cent of people own *almost half* of all capital, 500 times as much as 90 per cent of the people.[10]

Further, the few with most capital also have most *access* to the rest of society's capital, especially the savings that many small owners of capital have deposited in banks and pension funds. Most bank loans go to a few large capitalists because they are most able to afford the high interest rates. They therefore have the most use of capital other than their own.

This is an extremely important issue. It seems that we allow about 3 per cent of people to determine what most of our society's capital will be put to producing or developing. It also means that almost all of the unearned income, and the profits from society's invested capital, is going to perhaps 5 per cent or at most 10 per cent of the people. (See Chapter 9.)

How do you get rich?

Some people get rich by hard work and ability, but not that many. The best way to become rich is to arrange to have very rich parents; most wealthy people inherit their fortunes (two-thirds of Britain's wealthy people have done so).[11] But if this seems difficult for you to arrange now, there is another way.

Would you like to 'earn' $40 million in one day? How? It goes something like this. You stage a company raid by buying shares in a firm to take over control of it. The people who control the company by owning the biggest number of shares panic and start buying up more shares to make sure you do not build up a bigger holding than they have. You bid against them, buying more shares energetically. Because the demand for the shares is rising the price rises. When the right moment arrives you suddenly sell all the shares you bought... at a much higher price than you paid for them. Then you cry all the way to the bank about your failed takeover raid.

> 'Mesa Petroleum staged a takeover raid on Gulf Oil. Gulf shares rose from $41 to $80 in six months; Mesa suddenly sold its shares for a $760 million profit.
> Mesa has never succeeded in a takeover bid, but has made $13,000 million in its takeover raids.'
> R. Miller. 'The Hungriest Raider of All', in *Australian*, 27.12.85, p12.

Mr. Rupert Murdoch made $40 million from his failed takeover raid on Rank Xerox. The Australian entrepreneur, Robert Holmes à Court, failed in a dozen takeover bids but made millions of dollars from each. The takeover speculators borrow money to finance their raids but these sums can be deducted from their taxable incomes. They paid little or no tax in their speculative profits until a capital gains tax was introduced.

The conventional view is that takeovers are good because they involve an energetic entrepreneur taking over an inefficient company and improving its performance, thereby benefiting the whole economy. But it is by no means clear that in general a firm's performance is improved by a takeover. A study of Australian takeovers between 1970 and 1980 found that on average companies performed no better after takeover.[12]

What makes people poor?

It is widely held that people are poor either because they are lazy or do not have the ability to earn or manage money. In other words, 'It's their own fault.' Some people are indeed poor because they're lazy or stupid, but this isn't the reason why most poor people are poor. Societies like ours have lots of poor people *because social structures and rules create poverty.* This society takes many ordinary people and makes them poor. We have rules and procedures which determine that many people will be poor. The main ones are:

1 We have unemployment. When there is not enough work to keep all who want work employed for a full week, we take some people completely out of the workforce and condemn them to very low incomes, instead of sharing the problem among all of us.

2 We give miserly pensions to people who cannot earn. In the late 1980s all Australian pensions were under one-quarter of the average income, and under the poverty line.

3 Different jobs are associated with very different incomes. Some people who work solidly for a week take home much more money than others who work just as hard.

4 A great deal of income goes to richer people just because they have money; that is, in this society interest is paid on borrowed money, and a very few have most of the money available for borrowing. According to some estimates possibly 20 per cent of all the wealth created goes in this form to a tiny proportion of people. (See Chapter 9.) This is one of the most important rules by which our society proceeds and it is a rule which guarantees that there will be extreme inequality. (Many other societies not only have no such rule but regard this as an immoral procedure.)

5 The tax laws magnify inequality, when they are supposed to be the means whereby income is redistributed from rich to poor. 'But don't the rich pay a lot of tax?' Unfortunately, no they do not, and they are paying less as the years go by. The proportions of tax paid by corporations and rich people in developed countries have been falling for decades. Whereas organised crime costs the USA $7 billion a year, tax evasion by the rich costs $9 billion a year. In 1984, 40 US corporations with combined profits of $10 billion paid no tax at all.[13] Company tax in Australia fell from 18 per cent of all tax revenue in 1960 to 10 per cent in 1985.[14] Because there are so many loopholes for the rich to avoid tax, one taxation

inquiry concluded that 'taxation for the rich is voluntary' — they do not have to pay if they do not want to.[15] Another inquiry concluded that Australia's problem '… is not getting the rich to pay more tax, but getting them to pay any tax at all.'[16] The point is that '… rather than redistributing income to the poor … the tax laws … provide a vehicle for redistribution to the wealthy'.[17]

Inequality in our society is no mystery. There are many societies in which there is virtually no inequality in income or wealth. Our society has a lot of inequality simply because of the rules and structures built into it. The rules and procedures adopted by our society make some people rich and make many people poor.

Rich world — poor world: increased polarisation

The discussion in this chapter has dealt mostly with trends in inequality in the richest countries. When we compare rich and poor worlds we come to much worse conclusions. The gap between the rich and poor nations is huge and increasing rapidly. In 1960 the rich world's per capita income was 20 times that of the Third World; by 1990 the ratio was over 60 to 1. Each year rich world incomes rise on average about $400 while incomes for the poorest half rise $10, and incomes for hundreds of millions of people actually fall. Our economy attends mostly to the relatively rich, allocating investment and goods to those who can pay most. Consequently polarisation now appears to be taking place within the global economy at an accelerating pace.

Unemployment: incurable in this economy

Unemployment is the most important cause of poverty. It is a depressing comment on our society that any level of unemployment is accepted. Unemployment damages people: most rates of illness, breakdown and suicide are much higher for those out of work. Our society accepts that when we need less than the equivalent of all workers working full-time it is all right to dump some into the poverty and misery of total unemployment. A civilised society would not allow this to happen. It would ensure that all who wanted work would have a share of the work needed. Many societies do this, including the Israeli kibbutzim (self-governing settlements of around 400 people). So why don't we do it? Essentially because it doesn't suit employers, who prefer to be free to hire 90 workers full-time and leave ten unemployed rather than employ 100 for 90 per cent of the time. While the latter option would involve greater costs (e.g. for workers' compensation insurance), it would encourage people to argue that if workers are taking less income in order to share the burdens of less than full employment, employers should also help shoulder the burden by taking a cut in profits.

Before 1970 the official Australian unemployment rate was around 1 per cent. By the early 1990s it had climbed to around 10 per cent. However, the official figures are deliberately misleading and the magnitude of the problem is much greater than they would indicate. The figures only refer to people who are actively seeking work in the week the survey is taken. They omit people who have given up hope of getting a job. They count as employed the many people who work in a part-time job when they want full-time work. It is widely accepted that the real unemployment rate is up to twice the official rate.[16]

Over 30 million people were jobless in the rich countries in the late 1980s. Over one-fifth of young Australians were unemployed and many of them might never secure a permanent job. These large numbers of people could only become employed again if we were all to increase our per capita rates of consuming, yet as Chapter 6 emphasises, rich countries are causing catastrophic resource and environmental problems because they are already producing and consuming too much. We urgently need to reduce overall levels of production and consumption. Furthermore, in our economy the problem of unemployment has a strong tendency to become twice as bad every 35 years, because that is the approximate period in which productivity, i.e. output per worker, doubles. Obviously we do not have an economic system which can enable us to solve the unemployment problem in an ecologically sane way.

Automation: why is it a problem?

Automation should be something that we welcome because it reduces the need for humans to do boring work. Yet its development is a serious problem in our economy. Why? Because factories and offices are the private property of a few who operate them to make profits. When a business owner puts in automated plant he gets all the benefits from reduced labour costs, while workers get none; in fact many jobs are lost. Inevitably introduction of automation is a problem in such an economic system.

Consider what happens in a domestic economy when a family acquires a washing machine. This means less work for all, because the whole family owns the productive machinery under its roof and shares in the benefits. If all a country's citizens owned all that country's productive plant they would then welcome increased automation because it would mean less boring work for people to do and more benefits for all (such as more leisure time).

As with unemployment, no satisfactory solution to the automation problem is possible within this economy. In fact automation is one of the forces most likely to cause this economy to self-destruct. As more factories and offices are automated we will move closer to the situation where they produce all our goods and services without any labour, but then businesses will go bankrupt because no one will have a job and therefore no one will have the income to buy any of the goods and services produced, and we will all starve. Our economy only avoids this situation because the state gives considerable sums of money to people, such as poor people, so they can go on buying. However, this cannot be done unless many people do have jobs and are paying taxes to provide the money to transfer to those unemployed. If all businesses are automated no one will have an income on which to pay tax. This is a good illustration of what Marx termed the 'contradictions' built into the nature of capitalism.

What about job sharing?

Sharing the available work is of course desirable in principle but this can be of little value if the total amount of work required decreases markedly in the long term. What would happen to the economy if we reached the situation where we were sharing only 60 per cent of the work and income we have now? This economy could not tolerate such a reduction in demand.

Redistribution?

Most people discontented about inequality have wanted to tackle the problem by redistributing wealth and income from rich to poor. This can no longer be the essence of a satisfactory strategy because the resource and environmental costs involved in producing present volumes of output and wealth are unsustainable. Rich countries are producing and consuming at per capita rates that cannot be kept up for many more decades. Even if we were to redistribute this output dramatically, this would not change the total amount of economic activity, energy use or environmental impact. So a very different solution has to be sought. Chapter 12 will discuss how all might be guaranteed secure and satisfying lives despite far lower average income per capita than we have now in the developed countries.

Is the problem being solved?

Since 1980, inequality seems to have become much more acute in virtually all countries. In that time the 'wealth' created each year in most countries has increased by about one third, meaning that it would have been very easy to totally eliminate poverty. There are reasons for thinking that, as the years go by, inequality will increase.

Firstly, this economy attends mostly to the rich and to middle income earners, i.e. to those with capital and those with 'effective demand'. It will produce mostly what these groups want since that is most profitable. It will only develop those areas most likely to maximise profits. Two factors are especially important here. As time goes by, productivity increases and fewer workers are needed, so unemployment will tend to increase in the long run.

Secondly, the changes to the world's trading system being made through the General Agreement on Tariffs and Trade (GATT) conferences are sweeping away many of the controls governments once had for protecting their industries and markets for the benefit of their own people. From here on, large numbers of little producers and suppliers will be put out of work and many regions will decline as the giant corporations enjoy their new freedom to relocate plants to the lowest wage areas and buy from the cheapest suppliers, to drive small local producers out of operation and to sell to the highest bidders. Of course these GATT changes will do wonders for Gross World Product, but they will further impoverish billions of already poor people while greatly enriching the corporations and their well paid staff. There is likely to be an acceleration in the polarisation between rich and poor in the next few decades.

The solution?

The only way our present economic system can seek to solve the unemployment, poverty and inequality problems is by increasing production and consumption. Only if we use up more things can more factories open and employ more people. But as we have seen, the total amount of producing and consuming in rich countries is already far greater than is necessary to give good living standards to all. More importantly, it is far more than all the world's people could ever rise to.

No sensible answers to the problems of inequality, unemployment and poverty are possible in this economy. The only satisfactory solution is to move to an economic system in which it is possible to decide on the limited volume of production we need to provide comfortable living standards for all, to share the necessary work between all, and to share the resulting output. If it only takes 70 per cent of the available labour power to do this, then all workers should be able to work for only around 70 per cent of a full work week.

A most absurd and tragic aspect of the unemployment problem is that many people suffer boredom and even do without basic necessities when they and their local areas could be producing for themselves the things they need for a good quality of life. With a little organisation and a minimal amount of start-up capital they could immediately begin baking bread, producing fruit, vegetables and dairy products (from vacant city areas), and making basic furniture, clothing and footwear. But our economy will not facilitate such initiatives, because it makes almost all capital available to only the most profitable investment opportunities. Consequently we have the absurd situation where the living standards of people in a steel town depend on whether or not foreign corporations order more steel and so create jobs and incomes with which local people could pay for imported food, when those people could be happily engaged in producing from local resources most of the things they need!

As we shall see in the next chapter, satisfactory development must involve much more regional self-sufficiency, so that people in an area can spend most of their time producing to meet local needs. Such an economy need have no unemployment, because it could make sure that all who want work could share in production of the things needed in the area.

NOTES

1   Australian Bureau of Statistics, *Survey of Income and Housing Costs and Amenities*, (Cat. 6523), Canberra, 1990, p5.

2   J. Mangan, 'How the tax grab changed', in *Australian Society*, Nov. 1984, p8. C.J. De Vita, *America in the Twenty-First Century: A Demographic Overview*, Washington, Population Reference Bureau, May 1989. *Monthly Review*, Oct. 1986, p30. P. Watts, 'America's New Economy: A Basic Guide', in *Future Survey*, no.9, 1988, p473. P. Hawken, *The Next Economy*, Holt, Rhinehart and Winston, 1983, p86. S. Elliott, 'Wealth, income and poverty in Australia', in *ACTCOSS News*, 9, 5, Sept. 1994, pp1-23.

3   'In Whose Interest?' in *Newsletter*, no. 35, Sydney, Social Welfare Research Centre, December, 1985, p27.

4   V. Keegan, 'Economic Growth — for the benefit of the rich', in *The Guardian*, 14 June, 1987, p5. For the US decline, see J. Kloby, 'The Growing Divide: Class Polarization in the 1980s', in *Monthly*

Review, Sept. 1987, p5.

5 'The changing face of poverty', in *Australian Society,* February, 1986, p20. *Sydney Morning Herald,* 21 Sept. 1983, p1. 'Uniting Church', in *Economic Justice, The Equitable Distribution of Genuine Wealth,* Sydney, 1989.

6 Stated by the Social Policy Research Unit, Melbourne University, 23 April, 1989.

7 S. Elliott, 'Wealth, income and poverty in Australia', in *ACTCOSS News,* 9, 5, Sept. 1994, pp1-23.

8 P. Ekins, *The Living Economy,* London, Routledge and Kegan Paul, 1986, p234.

9 E. Edgar, *Australian Society,* 1980, p.73. See also 'Uniting Church', in *Economic Justice, The Equitable Distribution of Genuine Wealth,* Sydney, 1989, p5.

10 S. Brouwer, *Sharing the Pie,* The Big Picture Books, 1988. See also P. Ekins, *The Living Economy,* p.234; J. Kloby, *op cit.,* (note 4 above).

11 M. Campbell, *Capitalism in the UK,* 1981, p89. For similar conclusions on Australia see *Sydney Morning Herald,* 4 May 1985, p1.

12 See J.W. Brock, 'Bigness is the Problem', in *Challenge,* July-Aug. 1987, pp 11-16; F.M. McDougall and D.K. Round, 'The Determinants and Effects of Corporate Takeovers in Australia, 1970-1981', in *The Effects of Mergers and Takeovers in Australia,* Information Australia 1987, pp 11–16. However it has been found that takeovers result in higher share prices and some have interpreted this as better performance. This is a challengeable conclusion given that any takeover battle raises share prices. See P. Dodd, S. Bishop and R. Officer, *Australian Takeovers: The Evidence, 1972-1985,* Australian Graduate School of Management, University of NSW, 1987.

13 P. Grabosky, 'Ill-Gotten Gains', in *New Internationalist,* Dec. 1985, p15.

14 R. Henderson and D. Hough, 'Sydney's Poor Get Squeezed', in *Australian Society,* Nov. 1984, p22.

15 J. Mangan, *op. cit.,* p .9.

16 F. Stilwell, 'Where to Lay Tax Emphasis', in *Australian Society,* June 1985, p20.

17 J. Freeland and R. Sharp, *Capitalist Crisis and Schooling,* South Melbourne, Macmillan, 1986, p226.

7

Third World development

T HE UNSATISFACTORY NATURE of our economy is most clearly
apparent when we examine Third World development. Since
the early 1970s there has been considerable recognition in development literature that the global economic system and the
conventional approach to development are not only failing to solve
Third World problems but are actually their main causes. At first
sight it is quite implausible that pursuing economic growth could
possibly be the source of the problems. This chapter will explain that
when this is made the supreme goal of development the economy
prospers at the expense of most of the people.

Global inequality
Only about one-fifth of the world's 5.5 billion people live in developed countries. This fifth use at least three-quarters of the resources
sold each year, and their per capita resource-use rates are 15 to 20
times those of most other people in the world. The average US per
capita energy use is 55 times the average for the 80 poorest countries.
GNP per person in the rich countries is over 60 times that for the
poorest half of the world's people. And the gap is widening.

At least 1,000 million people live in severe poverty, without
adequate nutrition. According to Lean, Hinricksen and Markham,
half the people in the Third World do not have safe drinking water,
and water-borne diseases kill 25,000 people every day.[1] Goldsmith
and Hildyard state that 'between 9 and 22 million children less than
5 years old die each year because of lack of water, inadequate sanitary
facilities, and water-borne diseases'.[2]

Many Third World workers are paid an amount that would be
equal to $A25 a week while having to pay rich world prices for things
they buy. In a typical Third World country a tiny minority of people

Growth has brought few significant benefits to the Third World poor.
M. Todaro, *Economics for a Developing World*, New York, Longman, 1992, p160.

Three quarters of Latin American countries fell 10% in GNP per person in the 1980s ... For the poor, particularly in Africa and Latin America, the 1980s have been an unmitigated disaster, a time of falling earnings and rising debt, of falling food supplies and rising death rates.
G Lean, M.D. Hinricksen and A. Markham, *The Atlas of the Environment*, London, Arrow Books, 1990, p41.

Most Central Americans are worse off than they were 10 years ago.
CENTRAL AMERICA IN DIRE ECONOMIC STRAITS
Third World Network Features, no. 719, 1991.

36 nations are poorer today than they were a generation ago.
L.H. Summers, 'The Challenges of Development', in *Finance and Development,* March 1992, p6.

For 800 million people in 43 countries income has been falling for 10 years.
Worldwatch Institute, *Vital Signs,* Washington, 1993, p17.

We have seen three decades of development and for most of these countries the problem of mass poverty and unemployment has been aggravated, or ... appears to be intractable.
A. Rahman, 'People's Self-Development', in P. Ekins and M. Max-Neef, eds., *Real Life Economics,* London, Routledge and Kegan Paul, 1992, p171.

Today the great hopes placed in development have obviously been dashed. ...it became obvious around 1970, that the pursuit of development actually intensified poverty.
S. LaTouche, *In the Wake of the Affluent Society,* London, Zed Books, 1993, pp40, 29.

possess almost all wealth and power. In Latin America, for example, a mere 3 per cent of landowners own 70 per cent of the land and the rich minority often ruthlessly exploit the poor and crush any protest. No real improvement in the living standards of the poor is likely until these unjust conditions and social structures are changed.

The unsatisfactory state of development

The conventional 'growth and trickle down' approach to development has been pursued energetically in most of the Third World for at least 40 years. A great deal of development has taken place but little of it has benefited the poor majority. Although there have been considerable improvements in infant mortality and life expectancy on average, improvements in material living conditions for the poorest 40 per cent have in the 20 years to 1980 been quite disappointing. Third World debt has soared, obviously meaning poor countries are doing just the opposite of trading their way to prosperity. As the following statements indicate, conditions in general for most Third World people have probably deteriorated significantly during the last 10 to 15 years — while world economic output rose by more than one third.

The conventional approach to development

Conventional economic theory attributes Third World development problems to lack of education, capital and technology, to corrupt regimes, and to lack of 'modernisation'. The critical view is that although some of these internal factors are important, the basic problems exist because of the way the global economy inevitably works and because conventional development theory has been followed.

The conventional approach to development more or less identifies development with economic growth. It sets out to stimulate as much business turnover as possible in order to yield 'trickle down' benefits to all. However after forty years experience we can now see clearly some of the main outcomes and implications of this approach.

¤ *Development starts with the rich.* The few with capital are encouraged to invest it in order to make as much money as possible. Uneven development and inequality are the inevitable results. Small sectors centred on the capital cities typically boom but the rest of the country often remains more or less stagnant. The rich rapidly become much richer and those few regions able to yield most profit to investors prosper.

¤ *Very little ever trickles down to the poor!* This is evident in many studies on particular countries, and in overall world economic statistics. In fact, large numbers of poor people have their low living standards reduced through conventional development, for example when landlords terminate their leases in order to increase export crop plantations.

'Economic policies in India therefore have been designed to maximise output of goods and services and have assumed that the benefits of progress would diffuse automatically throughout the society ... Indian experience shows that the expected trickle down effect of economic development has not taken place.'

M. Karkal and S.I. Rajan, 'Progress in provision of basic human needs in India, 1961-1981', in *Economic and Political Weekly*, 23 Feb. 1991, p443.

☐ Even if trickle down were clearly solving the problems of the poor majority, at the present rate it would take *many decades* to make any significant difference. The rate of growth of GNP per capita has been slow, about 1.6 per cent p.a. At this rate it would take another 210 years before the poorest one billion of the world's people reached half the present level in rich countries. This is quite unacceptable, given that *all the resources needed to solve the main problems fairly quickly are available.* Robert McNamara, ex-president of the World Bank, has stated that even if the growth rate of the poor countries doubled, only seven countries would close the gap with the rich nations in 100 years. Only another nine would reach our level in 1,000 years. (Quoted in W.R. Thompson, ed., *Contending Approaches to World Systems Analysis,* London, Sage, 1983, p29.)

☐ *Developed countries grab most of the resources available* in the world because they can outbid the poor. They are therefore taking far more than their fair share and depriving millions of people of a sufficient share. For example Agarwal and Narain report, 'For every one hectare of land that a Dutch person uses in the Netherlands, that person uses about 5 hectares outside, and most of it in the Third World'.[3] A market system distributes scarce things according to who can pay most, not according to need. No mechanism is more responsible for the Third World's problems than this basic principle in our economic system.

☐ Conventional economic theory insists that it is most important for Third World countries to develop export industries, so that they can earn money for development. As a result Third World productive capacity is geared more and more to supplying the rich nations. Forests are cut and exported, and land is converted from producing food for local people to producing crops to export to the rich countries. Thus, Third World labour and capital are put into producing for consumers in rich countries and for the small rich groups within the Third World. The income goes mostly to owners of the factories and plantations and little of it to the majority of people. This is most disturbing with respect to the conversion of large areas of Third World land, always the best land, into the production of crops for export to the rich countries. More than 100 million ha are in this category, including more than half the best land in many countries where hunger is a major problem.

EXPORT CROPS

In San Salvador 'plantations now take up half of the total farming area of the country – including all the prime land.'
E. Goldsmith, 'Is Development the Solution or the Problem?', in *The Ecologist*, 15, 1985, p21.

'Asian countries are exporting increasingly more of their high yield food products which are still badly needed locally. The fertile valleys of Mindanao in the Southern Philippines, for example, are entirely devoted to banana and pineapple cultivation, which foreign multinationals process, pack and ship in refrigerated ships to Japan. None of it lands of the tables of the local population, which is among the poorest in South East Asia.'
G. Kent, 'The Food Trade: The Poor Feed the Rich', in *The Ecologist,* 15, 1985, 5/6, p236.

'A long list of examples could be given of countries with inadequately nourished populations which export agricultural products to richer nations... 4.4 million ha of Third World land produce food to be fed to animals in Germany.'
U. Ratsch and H. Diefenbacher, 'EEC Feedstuff Imports and Excess Production', in *Development*, 4, 19, 1985, p19.

European cattle are fattened on soya meal, quite edible by humans, half of it imported from Brazil and other Third World countries.
J. Seymour and H. Girardet, *Blueprint for a Green Planet*, 1987.

'In the Philippines ... 30% of the total cultivated land area is now given over to cash crop production for export...'
E. Goldsmith, 'Development as Enclosure', in *The Ecologist*, 22, 4, July/August 1992, p139.

Many Third World governments have developed heavily subsidised export industries by spending to develop infrastructures such as roads, ports and power supply. Countries compete in offering attractive conditions (including long tax holidays, low wages and lax safety and anti-pollution laws) to entice transnational corporations to invest. There is little evidence of how the eventual royalties and taxes from resource exports and free-trade manufacturing zones compare with these costs, but in many cases it is probable that the host country has actually lost on the deal; i.e. their infrastructure development costs have probably been *greater* than their receipts from royalties and other payments. (This could be true for some Australian export industries, notably woodchips and aluminium.[4])

¤ This conventional, 'maximise the growth of GNP' approach to development greatly benefits the local rich classes, the transnational corporations and the consumers in rich countries. Only a tiny share of the benefits go to those who do the work; wages in mines and plantations are often near starvation level. The things developed are those that people with capital can see will maximise their profits on their investments and these are never factories to produce what poorer people need. Governments encourage local and foreign capitalists to invest in what they wish because this is the most effective way to boost economic activity, and everyone takes it for granted that that is what development is all about.

¤ In other words *the wrong industries are developed.* What Third World people need and what they get from conventional development programs differ greatly. They need food and shelter and clean water, but instead they get tourist hotels, export plantations and car factories. Again, this is simply because in this economic system a few people have most of the capital and it is always far more profitable for them to invest in factories to produce goods for the rich than in providing necessities for the poor majority.

¤ The result is *inappropriate development.* This is an inevitable consequence of our economic system because it is always far more profitable to channel investment into producing what the rich want, and to sell the available resources to them. In other words *the global economy is extremely unjust.* It deprives Third World people not only of a fair share of the available world resources but it also deprives them of the resources in their own country. The local minerals are shipped out to the rich countries only yielding profits to a few local business people, and minuscule wages to the few who have jobs in the mines, etc.

It should be emphasised that what the conventional development theorists urge in an effort to get development going is precisely what will accelerate these disastrous effects. They insist that if there can be more economic turnover, more sales and more foreign investors enticed in, that will be development and it will by definition be 'producing more wealth for all to share'. The fact that the wealth created is largely inappropriate and mostly benefits the rich is ignored. Also ignored is the fact that, after decades of this approach and vast increases in aggregate economic wealth, the economic situation of the poor majority has not improved much and for many it has deteriorated.

The core fault built into the conventional approach to development is its failure to discriminate between desirable and undesirable forms of investment and productive activity. No conventional theorist every says, 'Here is a list of items only rich urban people could buy, mostly luxuries. Let's make sure they are *not* produced'. An appropriate development strategy would constantly involve decisions of this sort. Virtually all economists and politicians simply devote themselves to increasing the production of *anything* — i.e. anything investors would like to produce. They are not interested in whether or not the new factory is going to produce up-market handbags or another cosmetic. They are delighted when, as recently happened, an Australian firm wins a contract to export concrete garden gnomes to Japan. The conventional economic mind sees this as an unquestionably good thing because it will create more income, jobs, sales, taxes and national 'wealth'. A child could see that in a world with urgent resource scarcity problems, several billion deprived people and crumbling global ecosystems, to devote precious resources and talent to such purpose is morally repugnant.

When the purpose of development is taken to be doing whatever will maximise the rate of increase of economic activity, then many poor people will not only get little or no benefit, they will actually *be deprived of resources they once had*. For instance, their land will be drawn into export crops or flooded by a dam, their neighbourhoods will be ruined by freeway construction, and their jobs eliminated by the coming of the modern factory. Hence we can state possibly the most important of all economic laws, one which conventional economics never acknowledges — *growth deprives*. Growth often greatly increases the income of many, but it has a powerful tendency to make those who are in most need even poorer.

Increasing numbers of critics actually see development as a process whereby people enjoying traditional ways of life outside the cash economy are drawn into the global economic system. They are then made dependent on exporting to it and therefore on having to sell their labour and resources to the dominant few within the global economy, and forced to open their regions to access by corporations to minerals, forests and potential markets. Norberg-Hodge[5] describes how this process is starting in Ladakh, one of the few regions where a rich and satisfying way of life has not yet been destroyed by market forces.

The same mechanisms devastate the lives of millions of people in the richest countries, although its effects there are less savage and less obvious. Most people in the rich countries suffer working conditions, living conditions and social conditions that are far less satisfactory than they could have been had the huge productive capacity available been applied to building supportive communities, cooperative arrangements, easy-going and democratic work places and leisure-rich neighbourhoods. They too are the victims of extremely inappropriate development. The best developments for them and their neighbourhoods are not more freeways, McDonalds, supermarkets and television channels, but these are the things that are developed in an economy where development is defined in terms of what will do most to increase sales, returns on investment, and the GNP.

If you define development as economic growth, then you will get:
- production of the most profitable things
- therefore production for the local rich and for export to the rich countries
- Third World resources and productive capacity, especially land, drawn into production for the rich
- more inequality
- migration to cities, slums and destruction of rural life
- employment of relatively few people
- adoption of western living standards
- ecologically unsustainable development — i.e. development that is inappropriate to the needs of most people.

What about the NICs?

¤ A few Third World countries have achieved remarkable growth via the conventional approach, such as 'Newly Industrialising Countries' (NICs), Taiwan and South Korea, Hong Kong and Singapore. However, it is a serious mistake to regard these as showing that all can do the same. Of course those few countries which compete hardest in the export arena (in South Korea's case by enforcing probably the worst working conditions in the industrialised world), will win the very limited available markets. However, these four countries account for less than 2 per cent of Third World population, so it is most implausible that all the rest could prosper by manufacturing goods for export to the rich countries (already overconsuming in a world where extensive trade protection reflects the difficulty of selling all the exports produced). In any case the situation of the NICs in the early 1990s has become much less impressive, even in terms of conventional economic criteria, let alone quality of life factors.[6]

'They have too many children'

It is commonly assumed that Third World countries are kept poor because they have more children than they can provide for. However, this is a not the basic reason for poverty and underdevelopment.

Firstly, most countries where people are very poor have quite sufficient resources to provide for their needs. For example, India has twice as much farmland per person as England so it is not possible to explain hunger in India in terms of too many people per arable hectare.

More importantly, it is now understood that there are very coercive economic forces at work on poor people leading them to have many children.[7] When you know that you will only be looked after in your old age if you have surviving children, when you know that the infant mortality rate is high, and when you need as much labour as you can get on the family farm, then you are under very strong incentives to have many children. The population growth problem is therefore primarily due to poverty; if there were old age pensions and piped water in villages, the need to have so many children would be reduced.

This is not to deny that most Third World (and rich) countries are overpopulated or that the world might now be carrying 10 times as many people as can be sustained in the long term. Many Third World countries face extremely serious problems in relation to the numbers of people they will have to cope with in coming decades, especially in relation to their rapidly deteriorating soils and ecosystems. In some there are also strong cultural pressures towards having large families. However the main point being made here is to deny that the primary cause of Third World poverty and underdevelopment can be explained in terms of having too many children. The basic causes are to be found in the way the global economy works and in the behaviour of the rich countries. These produce the impoverished conditions which oblige poor people to have many children.

What is development?

Development, conventionally defined, has brought considerable benefits to many Third World people, but it has also been responsible for enormous suffering and destruction. It has stripped hundreds of millions of people from villages where life was often very humble and hard but secure and rewarding, and cast them into the squalor of urban slums or starvation wages in plantations and factories, while it has taken huge amounts of land and other resources and devoted them to the benefit of the rich few. This vast human catastrophe has essentially been due to the core assumption in conventional economic theory and practice; that sheer economic growth is (or is the key to) development — just do what will be most likely to increase production for sale and that will be best for all in the long run.

The first glaring mistake here is that what matters is *the development of a society, not just the development of an economy.* What about the satisfactory development of the political system, community, social cohesion, the ecology, culture and values, the arts and urban and rural geography? When economic development is made the supreme or sole goal most of these other systems are actually damaged. (See Chapter 8).

Secondly the growth of an economy is very different to the development of a satisfactory economy. The key question should be, *What form might a good, satisfying, just and humane economy take?* Conventional economists have nothing to say about questions like this; all they are interested in is seeing the size of the economy increase, seeing the volume of production (of anything) for sale increase. They are therefore incapable of discussing the possibility that reducing GNP or deciding not to produce and sell certain things, or agreeing to take some items out of the cash economy, might improve the economy.

The point becomes clearest when we think about the desirable development of our neighbourhood or household economies. Improving these would probably have nothing to do with increasing the amount of production for sale going on. The best things to develop in your neighbourhood might be more community gardens or meeting places for old people. In fact removing some factories and busy roads and thereby lowering the economic turnover of the area might be marvellous developments. Sometimes it makes sense to think about the further development of our household, although many of us would say there is no need for any further change. If you can think of desirable developments there, they will probably have nothing to do with increasing the amount of production for sale going on in your household.

Obviously the concept of development has to do with moving to some desirable state, meaning that sometimes that state has been achieved and there is no need to do any more developing, and meaning that the concept is quite distinct from merely growing bigger, let alone distinct from constant increasing production for sale.

These points highlight such obvious absurdities in conventional development thinking that it is difficult to understand why such a seriously defective and dangerous conception of development has been allowed to inflict great suffering on billions of people. Had we made sure that the discussion of development was about building 'good' societies, including 'good' as distinct from 'big' economies, and the highest possible quality of life, the catastrophes that conventional development has inflicted would not have occurred.

Chapter 12 argues for a conception of appropriate and sustainable development which denies that there is any need for a society to follow the conventional path through industrialisation, urbanisation, and affluent living standards. It argues that we could easily and quickly build those geographical, social and economic arrangements that would provide a high quality of life to all via relatively simple systems. Conventional economists cannot grasp this possibility since to them development can only be the very long and painful process whereby the expansion of production, sales, markets, industrialisation, foreign investment, trade, etc. eventually leads to the complete 'Losangelisation' of the entire planet. In other words, they only deal with capitalist development, i.e. with the path you would take if your goal was to maximise the amount of profitable business turnover and the opportunities for investment.

The implications of the limits to growth argument

The conventional approach to development proceeds on the assumption that there are enough resources left for us all to go on pursuing affluence and growth, and for the Third World to rise to high material living standards. But as has been explained in Chapter 5, current estimates of recoverable resources and environmental impacts leave *no possibility* of all people ever rising to the per capita resource levels the rich countries have now, let alone to the levels we will reach if our living standards continue to increase.

This point is extremely important for thinking about development. To date virtually everyone, including the most conventional
and the most radical theorists, have taken it for granted that the aim
is to raise the Third World to the sorts of living standards and
lifestyles and to the level of industrialisation the rich countries have.
But this is not possible in view of the globe's resource, energy and
environmental limits. From now on the goal of development (for rich
and poor countries) has to be to establish satisfactory ways of life on
very low levels of resource use and GNP per person. For the Third
World this means building highly self-sufficient village and regional
economies minimally dependent on export, foreign investment or
capital-intensive technologies.

Again, it should not need to be emphasised that no significant
move in this direction is possible within the present economic system
which requires a constant increase in the volume of production and
consumption going on.

> 'The Third World cannot conceivably attain the sort of affluence that
> we know today in the affluent world.'
> E. Goldsmith and N. Hildyard, *Battle for the Earth*, London, Child and
> Associates, 1988, p133.

The inescapable conclusion: We must 'de-develop'

No solution to these problems is possible unless the rich countries
cease hogging so much of the world's wealth. We should move to ways
of life that permit Third World people to have a greater share of the oil
and the other resources available and to put more of their own land,
labour and capital into producing for themselves the things they need.

Hence we come again to the conclusion which sums up the situation so effectively: *'The rich must live more simply so that the poor may
simply live'*.

We have an empire

The foregoing discussion has explained how unjust the global
economy is. It delivers most of the world's wealth to the rich because
it allows market forces and effective demand to determine resource
distribution and development priorities. Our living standards in rich
countries are as high as they are largely because the global economy
is unjust. We could not have such affluent lifestyles if we were not

getting most of the resources, importing raw materials and goods produced for very low wages in the Third World, selling consumer goods to Third World elites, making high profits from foreign investment and loans to the Third World, etc., and gearing much Third World productive capacity to our demand. What would your food, beverages or clothing cost if those who produced them in the Third World were paid fair wages?

The rich countries do not steal from poor countries or take things from them by force. We get much of the wealth produced in the Third World through the normal operation of the global market economic system. We get most of the resources for sale by outbidding those who need them most. We get the labour of the Third World applied to our purposes, because many of the enterprises set up are factories and plantations producing for us. The Third World's capital and land produce for us because that is the most profitable purpose for its owners to put it to.

We could not have such high living standards as we do have without the empire that is made up by all the countries in which our corporations can do so much profitable business. Just imagine our situation if the Third World had opted for an approach to development based on a minimum of involvement with rich countries, rejecting foreign investment and trade. We would then not have access to their land, capital or cheap labour and could not gear these to producing things for us.

Of course we pay for what we get from the Third World, but almost all the payment goes to the few who own the plantations and factories. We and they are the beneficiaries of a grossly unjust economic system that has developed little more than those industries gearing Third World productive capacity to our benefit. The other main way we benefit is by being able to sell luxury consumer goods to the Third World's rich, who pay for them with income derived from the export factories and plantations they own.

The important issue here is not whether or not there is a net flow of wealth from the poor to the rich world, although there usually is on a number of accounts. These include trade, falling terms of trade, patents and licences, repatriated profits on foreign investment, capital flight, brain drain and hidden transfer payments by corporations. Especially disturbing are loan repayments to banks. In the later years of the 1980s these represented a net flow of approximately $30 billion p.a. from poor countries; i.e. interest payments on debt. In addition the money that flows out as profits on foreign investment each year can be two or three times greater than the money that flows in.

But what matters far more than the net flow of money is whether or not the development that is taking place is appropriate. When development is conceived in conventional terms, then large volumes of capital are crucial by definition, since development equals increase in productive capacity measured in dollar value. However, not much wealth or capital is needed for appropriate development to take place (although land is needed). It might not matter much if a considerable net amount of wealth flowed from a Third World country if at the same time appropriate development were taking place, building the village gardens, stores, windmills and forest gardens that would enable people to have low but satisfactory material living standards, robust community organisations, a sustainable ecosystem, democratic local control, and thriving and secure locally self-sufficient economies. The most tragic fact about the current development scene is not that wealth is flowing from poor to rich but that little if any of the available land, labour or capital is going into appropriate development.

Repression is required

Because the trickle-down approach results in the enrichment of the rich and the deprivation of the poor, it is not surprising that serious discontent arises and sometimes rebellion erupts. In many Third World countries ruling classes can only keep 'order' by resorting to repression, sometimes relatively mild (such as banning unions), but often quite brutal.

This development approach is therefore directly connected to dictatorship and repression in the Third World. The rich countries have assisted numerous dictatorships and nasty regimes in repressing their peoples. They provide the aid and especially the military equipment to keep these rulers in power and keep their countries to the desired development strategies. To protect its global interests the United States has in recent decades maintained around 500,000 troops in 250 overseas military bases. Rich countries have often invaded to prop up or bring down governments.

The rich western countries need huge military machines to guarantee their continued access to most of the world's resources, especially to 'our' oilfields in the Middle East. We must have aircraft carriers and rapid deployment forces ready to be flown into the oilfields should any guerilla movement or regional conflict seem likely to cut our access to oil.

'...Third World regimes friendly to the United States are likely to be reactionary and repressive; no democratic government could permit its country's resources to be developed on terms favourable to American corporate and government interests... It is no accident that America's closest allies in the Third World are among the worst authoritarian regimes; South Korea, South Africa, Indonesia, Brazil and Taiwan.'
I. Katznelson and M. Kesselman, *The Politics of Power*, 1983, pp234-5.

'In Latin America, as elsewhere, "the protection of our resources" must be a major concern... The main threat to our interests is ... posed by nationalistic regimes that are responsive to popular pressures for immediate improvement in the low living standards of the masses.' p49.
Latin America's function was 'as a source of raw materials and a market. The threat of independent development was largely aborted.' p53.
'The major policy imperative is to block indigenous nationalist forces that might try to use their own resources in conflict with US interests.' p54.
'What matters is to bar independent development and the wrong priorities. For this purpose it is often necessary (regrettably) to murder priests, torture union leaders, "disappear" peasants, and otherwise intimidate the general population.'
N. Chomsky, *Deterring Democracy*, London, Verso, 1991

'With unfailing consistency, we (the US) have since the end of the Second World War intervened on behalf of conservative and fascist repression against revolution and radical reform... We have become the foremost counter-revolutionary status quo power on earth.'
M. Clark, *Ariadne's Thread*, London, Macmillan, 1989, p421.

It should be noted that the Soviet Union also controlled an empire, although its purpose seems to have been security rather than extracting wealth, and the scale of its operations seems to have been much smaller than that of the west.[8]

Western intervention has usually been justified on the grounds of helping a friendly government to defend itself against communist takeover. Even when this has been the case however, the cause of the trouble has usually been decades of exploitation, deprivation and repression from which local elites and the rich countries have benefited. In Central and Latin America, it is especially clear that revolutions have not been due to communism. As Blazier says, 'In

Central America the revolutionary parties are led by non-communists.'[9] He goes on to attack US governments for mistakenly claiming that communist parties have caused revolutions in Latin America.[10]

It is important for the rich countries that any attempt at an alternative path to development should fail. They have often gone to extraordinary lengths to destroy such efforts.

Terrorism

Resort to terrorism usually evokes outrage on the part of the rich countries. What is not acknowledged is that *the rich countries sponsor most of the terrorism carried out in the world.* The US and the USSR have been by far the worst offenders, providing the funds, training and arms used by many brutal Third World regimes to put down dissent. Compared to the toll from this state-organised terrorism, extremist groups such as the Palestine Liberation Organisation who might occasionally hijack aircraft and plant bombs in cities account for only a small fraction of terrorist activity.[11]

The solution: self-sufficient development

Factors other than global economic injustice contribute to the Third World's unsatisfactory condition, notably difficult climates, corrupt

---

SUPPLYING REPRESSION IN GUATEMALA

- Between 1950 and 1970, 3213 Guatemalan police and army personnel were trained under the US military assistance program.
- Between 1970 and 1975, 161 Guatemalan military personnel received training at the US Army School of the Americas, in the Panama Canal Zone.
- Between 1950 and 1976, Guatemala received a total of $74.6 million in US military assistance.
- Between 1961 and 1973, Guatemala received $4.85 million in US assistance to its police force.
- Between 1973 and 1976, the USA supplied 1120 revolvers, 640 carbines and 160,000 cartridges to the Guatemalan National Police.
- Between 1970 and 1975, there were around 15,000 death squad victims in Guatemala (Amnesty International estimate).

Michael T. Klare, *Supplying Repression: Support for Authoritarian Regimes Abroad,* Institute for Policy Studies, Washington 1977.

and incompetent governments and lack of expertise. However, it is increasingly accepted that satisfactory Third World development is impossible unless the rich countries cease taking so much of the world's wealth and permit Third World productive capacity to meet Third World people's needs, and therefore unless the conventional development model is scrapped. Alternative development theory is also based on the firm conviction that in almost all cases Third World countries have quite sufficient resources to sustain appropriate development. As Korten says, 'With few exceptions it is within the means of Southern countries to meet these needs for their own people — if their resources are so organised and used.'[12]

Following are the key elements in the conception of appropriate development increasingly being discussed in the alternative development literature.

◻ *Aim at sufficient, comfortable material living standards,* on the lowest reasonable per capital rate of use of non-renewable resources. Any idea of the affluent, industrialised living standards of the rich countries as the goal of development must be completely abandoned.

◻ *Reject GNP growth as an index of development* and do not confuse growth with development. In other words, *discriminate.* Don't just try to increase the amount of economic activity going on. Produce and develop only those things that are appropriate, first to meet the urgent needs of the poor majority and second to maintain all people at a low yet sufficient material living standard. Prevent development that would maximise growth if it would be inappropriate development. Ask whether satisfactory development of the whole society is taking place: ignore whether or not the GNP is growing.

◻ The single most important principle must be to *build highly self-sufficient village economies,* whereby most of the things the village needs can be produced by its people or produced locally using surrounding resources, especially forests and gardens. This means importing as little as possible from the national economy, and therefore reducing to a minimum the need to export to it. Identify the items the village or region is importing but could produce for itself.

◻ *Promote grassroots and participatory development.* Help local people to identify and work on local problems.

◻ *Ensure ecological sustainability,* especially by making the local forests and water catchments into abundant and permanent sources of food and materials.

◻ *Mostly use intermediate, labour-intensive technology,* instead of capital and energy-intensive high technology. It is impossible for all, or even for many, countries to have heavy industrialisation. However, use medium and high technologies in those (relatively few) places where they are appropriate.

◻ *Use cooperative strategies;* for example, community forests, shared workshops, cooperatives and village working bees. Think especially about providing 'free' communal goods and services, such as commons and village forests.

◻ *Minimise economic relations with the rich countries.* Import as little as possible, thereby reducing to a minimum the need to export. Borrow as little as possible and do so only for essential purposes. Do not permit importation of luxuries, or of items that can reasonably be produced locally. Only permit foreign investment if it is going to facilitate appropriate development.

◻ *Aim to achieve only sufficient material development,* culminating sooner rather than later in a zero-growth economy with a relatively low GNP per capita (although it might be quite desirable for selected industries to grow for a long time).

◻ *De-emphasise mere economic development.* Focus more on development of community, of village decision making procedures and especially of the local ecosystem. Think carefully about the point at which the village has had enough merely-economic development, i.e. enough production for sale. Think especially about developing sources of gifts, mutual assistance and free communal goods and services.

There is great and largely unrecognised scope for ordinary people in even the poorest countries to meet their own basic needs, if they are given access to productive resources, especially land. It is most disturbing that billions of people are condemned by conventional economic development theory to decades of deprivation when appropriate development strategies could enable the poorest people to provide themselves with satisfactory (though modest) living standards in at most a few years.

NOTES

1 G. Lean, D. Hinricksen and A. Markham, *The Atlas of the Environment,* London, Arrow Books, p41.

2 E. Goldsmith and N. Hildyard, *Battle for the Earth,* London, Child and Associates, 1988, p81.

3 S. Agarwal and S. Narain, *Towards Green Villages,* New Delhi, Centre for Science and Environment, 1989, p1.

4 J. West, in *Simply Living,* 2, 13, 1987, p48.

5 H. Norberg-Hodge, *Ancient Futures: Learning from Ladakh,* San Francisco, Sierra Club, 1991.

6 W. Bell and R. Broad, *The Crisis of the NICs: Fundamental, Not Transitional,* Briefing Paper 24, Canberra, Aust. Development Studies Network, ANU, Jan. 1992.

7 T. Trainer, *Developed to Death,* London, Green Print, 1989, p29. W. Murdock, *The Poverty of Nations,* Baltimore, Johns Hopkins University Press, 1980, pp82, 37, 58, 63. M.P. Todaro, *Economic Development in the Third World,* New York, Longman, 1985, p89.

8 R. Sivard, *World Military and Social Expenditures,* Virginia, World Priorities, Inc., 1981. Some 27 interventions by western governments since 1945 are listed in *New Internationalist,* Oct. 1978, p5.

9 C. Blazier, *The Giant's Rival,* Pittsburgh, University of Pittsburgh Press, 1983, p132.

10 Blazier, *op. cit.,* p153. P. Berryman makes the same point in *Inside Central America,* New York, Pantheon, 1985, p21.

11 E.S. Herman, *The Real Terror Network,* Boston, South End Press, 1982.

12 D.C. Korten, 'Sustainable Development: Growth vs Transformation', duplicated ms, Nov. 1991, p24.

8

The economy's impact on society

A SOCIETY IS MADE up of many things, including a political system, a moral code, a geography, customs and culture, as well as an economic system. Ideally all these should be important in determining what happens in a society, but in our era economic considerations are overwhelmingly dominant. Nothing is given anywhere near as much weight as what is 'good for the economy', and nothing has more influence on social change than economic development. Conventional economic thinking assumes and often asserts that what is good for the economy is good for society in general. Raising the GNP is defined as raising 'living standards'. Little attention is given to the fact that the 'progress' of our economy has seriously damaging effects on other crucial aspects of our society. Indeed it will be argued in this chapter that economic growth is the major factor undermining community, citizenship, social bonds, morality and the psychological and spiritual welfare of individuals in our society.

The moral quality of our economic system

Most of the moral values inherent in our economic system are quite despicable. The system is driven by greed and selfishness and it is basically predatory. Adam Smith, a most influential advocate of free enterprise, was struck by the fact that the system harnessed such undesirable motives, although he thought that somehow they would work to the benefit of all.

Firstly, what are the positive moral qualities that could be claimed for our economic system. The following might be listed.

¤ 'It encourages hard work'. Yes, but too much work and production take place now.

- ¤ 'It encourages thrift'. Not any more. What the system now requires more than anything else is as much spending and consuming as possible. The system now depends heavily on spending more than our income, i.e. it thrives on debt, not thrift.

- ¤ 'It encourages enterprise and effort'. Yes, but for undesirable reasons; i.e. to get rich or to avoid poverty, not to enjoy working to produce things to help people.

- ¤ 'It encourages rational thinking and efficiency'. Yes, but only in the narrow framework of the business's balance sheet. The system is extremely irrational and inefficient in allocating resources, investment and wealth according to human needs.

- ¤ 'The freedom of the individual is respected'. Yes, there is a considerable freedom for the individual to produce, work and buy as s/he wishes, although there are some savage limits too: unemployed people are not free to work. There could be much freedom of enterprise in a satisfactory society based on small local firms. However, at present there is far too much freedom of enterprise in the sense that market forces are given too much power to decide development and distribution.

Now let's consider some of the undesirable moral values required by or reinforced by our economy.

- ¤ It is all about individual acquisitiveness. The capitalists' purpose is to increase the income from his or her ventures. Workers want to receive as much income as possible for themselves and their families. There is no incentive for people to work for the good of the whole community as there is in a tribe where the common welfare depends on cooperative effort.

- ¤ It is all about greed. It is driven by the desire for greater individual enrichment. An ever-increasing GNP and ever-higher living standards are demanded, even in the richest countries.

- ¤ It is all about beating others in competition, not about cooperating and caring for others. Capitalism is a predatory system; it encourages and requires people to prey on each other. It is all right to take business from your competitors, even to bankrupt them. If they have to sell out, you drive a hard bargain. If they have financial problems, you take them over. If they are desperate for something you have, you know you can squeeze a higher price out of them.

- ¤ There is strong incentive for deceit and cheating. Sellers often deceive buyers as to the quality of the goods on sale.

¤ You grab as much as you can get. If something costs you only $5 and you can sell it for $20 you do so, unless someone else offers you $25.

WAS THIS A NICE THING TO DO?

Rupert Murdoch bought 3.5 million *Herald and Weekly Times* shares at an average price of $4 in a campaign to take over the company. He then decided to abandon the takeover attempt, and about an hour before this became known he sold the shares at $5.52, yielding a profit of $5 million. The sale was made in the knowledge that as soon as people realised the takeover was abandoned the scramble for shares in the company would cease and the price would fall, leaving the buyers with a huge loss. The price immediately fell to $4.15.

Figures taken from *Sydney Morning Herald*, Nov. 23 1979, p.17.

The need for a moral economy

Clearly, a major problem with our economic theory and practice is that they leave little place for morality. Many extremely important decisions affecting people's welfare are made without reference to what would be morally acceptable. They are made solely on the basis of what will make most money. It has been argued above that there are many other, usually much more important factors, such as what things humans need, what developments would build better communities and political systems, what would preserve cultural uniqueness, and especially what would maximise ecological sustainability. Decisions which maximise returns to owners of capital often have adverse effects in several or all of these areas, yet in our economy this factor is allowed to determine what is done. No other economic system humans have ever developed has functioned in this way. All previous economies ensured that 'moral' factors, such as social customs setting a 'just price', were the main determinants of economic activity. Market forces and the profit motive were typically given little or no role.

Our present economic system and the theory which underlies it obscure the great misery they cause. They deceive us into accepting grossly inhuman consequences. Several sections of this book explain how our economic system is the main factor producing the hunger and deprivation suffered by hundreds of millions of people. Yet this causal connection is not well understood, because we have been led to believe that the market system is natural, efficient and desirable, and that it 'rewards factors of production in proportion to their contributions'. This prevailing ideology leads most people to believe that we are not exploiting the Third World and we are not causing hunger; we are only trading with them, investing and doing normal business. As Bookchin says, '...our present economy is grossly immoral... The economists have literally "demoralised" us and turned us into moral cretins'.[1]

Similarly, economic theory claims that when an item becomes scarce its price rises automatically, as if this is a law of nature independent of human will. In fact, the price rises only because individual sellers eager to maximise their income put it up as quickly as they can. Our economic theory obscures the fact that it is not scarcity but human greed which makes prices rise.

Above all, economic theory leads us to think that the supremely important goal is to 'get the economy going', to stimulate growth. The fact that this siphons wealth to the rich, deprives the poor, develops the wrong industries and in the Third World starve millions is obscured.

The conserver economy sketched in Chapter 12 allows the market a role, but only a minor one, and it ensures that much weight is given to considerations to do with what is good for people, societies and ecosystems.

Work: destroyed in our economy

One of the saddest facts about our economy is that it has made work into an unpleasant burden for many people. Most work is not perceived as enjoyable or rewarding in itself. Many people hate their work and most only work for the money they receive. Our economy offers only 'alienated labour' or the 'factory mode of production', i.e. work characterised by:

¤ *Intense division of labour:* each worker performs only one small task again and again all day.

¤ *Hierarchy of power:* workers are ordered from above.

¤ *Factory regularity and discipline:* you work to the factory or office whistle, not when you feel like it.

¤ *No control over the process:* workers simply do what they're told.

¤ *No connection with the tools or the product:* workers neither own the means of production nor distribute the product nor see people enjoy it.

◻ *Extrinsic motivation:* you work only for the pay packet, not for the satisfaction of doing the job.

Work, and travelling to and from it, take up a large proportion of our adult waking lives. All that most people get for this is money. The time does not even pass pleasantly; it is endured. This is a tragedy because work could be quite different. The boredom of work is one of the main factors lowering the quality of life in rich countries.

Why has work been organised in these ways? Why has work been destroyed by the 'factory mode of production'? The answer is that the way work is to be organised is decided by people whose only concern is to make production costs as low as possible, which is achieved by using the factory mode of production. Boring, alienated labour is an extremely serious social and psychological cost inflicted on most people by this economic system because it suits the few who own the factories. Of course it results in cheaper goods, but this economy denies us the possibility of deciding whether we'd prefer to pay more for our goods in order to have more relaxed and pleasant work conditions. It would be very easy to organise a totally different work experience, but only within an economic system where maximising output per dollar of labour cost to the factory owner was not allowed to be the sole determining factor.

Marx and others have argued that work should not only be satisfying, it should also help us to grow as persons, to become more knowledgeable, thoughtful, skilled, valued, respected and humane individuals. Although this may sound strange to people who have grown up in an industrial society, we could reorganise work to achieve these aims, but only by totally remaking our economic system and adopting a quite different set of values. In Chapter 12 it is argued that instead of working about 35 hours a week for wages in factories and offices, eight hours a week working for money might suffice in a reorganised, 'conserver' society. Consider the wisdom of many tribal societies which produce just enough to satisfy their simple material needs on much less than the work-time we put in. People who live in hunter-gatherer tribes only spend two or three days a week 'working' and part of this is fun and adventure, like hunting.[2]

The socialisation effects

Surely the most important factor of all in a good society is the value system built into the hearts of its members. They will feel strong 'bonds' to others, to institutions, to traditions and moral principles. Ideally these bonds are not burdens but are positive, like the bonds of affection between two people whereby one feels that they not only ought to, but wants to, care for the other person. We cannot expect to have a caring, civil, safe, enlightened, cultured and sensible society unless certain desirable values predominate in the individuals who make up the society.

There are today serious concerns about the extent to which desirable values are being socialised in young people within western society, especially because within the last generation smaller family sizes, working mothers and the decline of community have come to mean that a narrower range of adults interact with children. As well, drugs and violence have become much more evident problems, unemployment has undermined the spirit of large numbers of people, the media have trivialised issues, the public life of the citizen has given way to private living and political apathy, things are left to the professionals, the corporations and the government, and films now present horrific violence as entertainment. 'The loss of community is finding expression with a vengeance in crime, drugs and vandalism.'[3]

Again the economy must take considerable responsibility for these effects, since profits are often maximised by the most trivial media content, by violent films and by goading people to consume and to indulge their individual wishes and by seducing them into passive dependence on corporations and bureaucracies. Only one of the seven deadly sins, laziness, is still regarded as clearly immoral. Our economy casts most if not all of the others as virtues — notably greed, envy and pride.

Market forces destroy society

Our society has made a serious mistake in allowing economic activity to become supremely important. It is now a highly commercialised society, permitting many things to be determined by monetary or cost/benefit calculations and by bids within a market. It will be argued in this section that there is a zero-sum or reciprocal relation between market relations and desirable social relations; the more that market relations develop between people, the more that desirable social relations will be driven out.

The degree to which we have based our society on market exchange becomes clearer when we examine the situation that existed in most societies throughout history, and in societies like ours until about 300 years ago. In almost all previous societies economic activity was determined mostly, and usually entirely, by social rules and procedures, not by the market. What a person produced, what he or she was paid, the price of the object, hours of work and who the work was done for, were all decided mainly by custom and tradition. We now settle almost all such matters by bargaining in the market place to maximise individual advantage, or by what will be most profitable to individuals.

Until about three hundred years ago there were very few markets and merchants and they were of quite minor importance. Most production and distribution were not determined by what would be most profitable, but rather by rules set by tradition, the church or organisations such as guilds. These non-market procedures set 'fair prices'. Labour, land, and capital were not sold. They were exchanged but the arrangements made were determined by social rules and not by bargaining in a market for the highest bid. 'Moral' considerations governed production and distribution. Decisions about production, investment and exchange were made in terms of what was considered to be proper, legal, traditional, inappropriate, sacred or just. This does not mean that the decisions were what we would now regard as the best ones. Often they would have reflected differences in power and at times would have resulted in outcomes we would regard as unjust.

It is therefore quite mistaken to assume that humans have always been motivated primarily by profit or have always had a market economy, or that such an economy is the natural, or the only way to organise economic affairs. In fact, virtually all previous societies (and all remaining 'primitive' societies) had exactly the opposite economic philosophy to ours.[4] The basic idea in our economy is to maximise one's own gain or advantage, for example when something is sold or bought. Anthropologists suggest that in almost all other economic systems that humans have developed over several thousand years the basic principle was actually *giving* things away. The hunter brought back a beast and gave it to the tribe, knowing that others had collected fruits and seeds and would give some of them to him. Goods and services were produced and given to others according to elaborate rules of 'reciprocity' whereby the recipients were bound to perform other services at some other time. The motive for producing was not primarily selfish; it was to benefit the recipient, a member of one's own tribe or town.

This is, of course, the way your household economic system works. Parents do not make sandwiches to sell to their children in order to maximise profits. They do it because they want to feed their children. Because this basis for production and exchange is so very different from that underlying our economy, people often find it hard to accept that the way we currently do things is historically most unusual.

Before the seventeenth century money lending for interest was immoral, it was expected that prices would be 'just', personal gain and hoarding were discouraged, work was for the 'well-being of the soul' and to produce things for direct local use not to make profit. Throughout most of history food, clothing and shelter and other basic resources were produced for use value and were distributed within tribes and groups on a reciprocal basis. The motive of individual gain from economic activities was generally absent; the very idea of profit, let alone interest, was either inconceivable or banned... Economies were organised in terms of central stores into which produce was placed, for later redistribution according to needs, prestige etc., but not purchasing power. Private property was justified only to the extent that it served the welfare of all.
F. Capra, *The Turning Point*, 1982, pp201-202.

By about the sixteenth century European society had changed to an economy in which the market was given great power to determine what happened. It has been argued that this was the most significant transformation in modern social history, and that it was a catastrophe.[5] It certainly released powerful productive forces, freeing entrepreneurs from the restrictions of custom. The problem, however, is that the more that economic transactions are determined by the market, the less that events can be regulated by social and moral considerations. When there were traditional rules about a fair day's pay workers received that pay, but when wages are set solely by bargaining in a market workers can be forced to accept starvation wages.

By permitting the market to take over so many functions we have allowed social traditions, bonds, customs and moral values to fade away as factors determining the distribution of goods and services. The concern here is not just that the market does many undesirable things to people (e.g. deprives the poor), but that our humanity and the richness of our culture and social interaction are diminished as more and more events and interactions come to be governed by impersonal and selfish marketing calculations.

If two friends exchange something they take into account what would be a fair price, and each considers the other's welfare. For example, the seller would point out possible faults in the object. These moral considerations do not arise if the thing is simply sold in a market. If you run out of sugar and go next door to borrow some, this creates and reinforces social relations. You renew an acquaintance, chat about local events, create bonds of gratitude and debt, think about your neighbour's help after the event, and you plan to return the favour. However, if you merely buy sugar from the supermarket this transaction creates or reinforces none of these social relations.

The powerfully destructive effects of market forces become clear when we imagine what would happen if they were allowed to determine events in the domestic economy. Possibly 40 per cent of all the real productive activity in our society actually takes place in this sector, but is ignored by economists because they are only interested in production for cash sale. What happens in this household economy is determined by cooperative and moral forces and by political processes, by reasoned discussion, by feelings and non-rational factors, by mutual concern, by voluntary inputs and reciprocity, and almost never by calculations of cash cost and benefit. Someone makes the toast and gives it to the others, while someone else is setting the table. Now imagine what would happen if we allowed all this economic activity of the household to be determined by market forces. That is, imagine having everything that someone produced or did for someone else sold. Mum might make the toast and sell it to the highest bidder. One result would be that the children wouldn't get much, if any. Dad would get it because he could bid more. People would have to compete against each other for scarce things, whereas at present they cooperate. All contributions would be calculated in terms of likely individual cash gain rather than willingly given to benefit the family. Moral considerations, such as 'Johnny should get a share of the toast because he needs food too, even though he can't pay much for it', would be overwhelmed by considerations to do with which transactions would make most profit.

Clearly it would be disastrous to allow merely marketing relations, calculations of monetary cost and benefit, to have any role in determining the basic functioning of the domestic economy. That economy is rightly determined by non-cash values and rules, most of which are altruistic and collectivist. To change to marketing relations would be to ensure that selfish motives predominated and that a competitive climate existed. To introduce such relations to a household would clearly be to destroy its *social* relations, or at least to drive out just about all of the desirable social relations and replace them by competitive, selfish, and predatory relations.

The more we strive to maximise production and consumption, i.e. GNP, the more we diminish the role for social relations and turn them into market relations. Purely selfish considerations will increasingly replace the moral and social considerations that are always involved in exchange. A market situation makes you quite selfish; you must focus on getting the best deal for yourself and you are definitely not encouraged to think about what might be best for others or for your community. Similarly, when sheer economic growth is the top social priority and commerce provides more and more things, people tend to do less for themselves and for each other outside the cash economy.

Mobility is another factor destroying social bonds. As industrial society developed, the need for a highly mobile workforce gradually emerged. When a new plant opens workers must be able to move to it. However, mobility tends to disrupt social connectedness. People cannot 'put down roots' in a community if they are constantly moving on to find work. (On average each US family moves every five years.)

This need for mobility has helped produce the nuclear family; mum, dad and the kids but no other relatives living under the same roof or nearby. This sort of family is well suited to an industrial society's need for workers who can move to new locations readily, but it is a very vulnerable and problem-ridden arrangement. It requires each adult to provide the other with everything that could once be obtained from many members of the extended family or tribe, such as advice, entertainment, affection, help. Should some misfortune befall one of the two adults the whole family is in trouble. It is a fragile and stressed arrangement and it is not surprising that there is such a high rate of family breakdown. People living in extended families and tribes have far more support.

Rural decline

In the rich countries the destructive impact of the economy on society is most dramatically evident in the decline of rural life. Thousands of farming families have to leave the land every year, resulting in the slow death of country towns and immense personal hardship. In the last 20 years the suicide rate for rural youth in Australia has multiplied by five. This economy does not need more than a few people in rural areas. It is much more 'efficient' to produce food on giant corporate farms with high-tech machinery that needs little labour, using inputs trucked in from transnational agribusiness corporations, and trucking the food out to the international market. If it's good for the economy we allow it to happen. Therefore there is no possibility of us deciding to preserve rural life because it is in principle desirable, permitting some people to live at their own pace and be masters of their own small farms and members of cohesive small communities even though they cannot produce food as cheaply as agribusiness corporations can. To do that would of course be to lower our 'living standards', because we would be paying more for agricultural products from these less efficient farmers. In this society, that settles the issue; we just do what is most economically efficient. In a sane economy we would be able to discuss and decide whether it was best for people in general and especially for the ecology of rural areas to maintain small farming as a way of life in view of all the non-cash economic factors that should be taken into account.

Keeping the economy in its place

The main argument of this chapter is that there are many more important considerations than those to do with the cash sector of the economy. We have made a serious mistake in allowing these narrow economic criteria to be the most important determinants of what happens in our society. Often we should do what is best for the town, or for some sections of the community, or for the environment, or do what makes the workplace pleasant, or what will share work more evenly, or what is just and right, even though this will not be the cheapest or the most economically efficient option.

The insistence on the supremacy of cranking up the cash economy is most apparent in 'economic rationalism'. A top Canberra economic bureaucrat recently defined his craft in these terms; 'Economic rationalism means removing impediments to economic activity'.[6] What matters to him is increasing the volume of business turnover or production for sale and anything that interferes with this is in principle undesirable. Michael Pusey's study of these bureaucrats stresses the way they see the economy as the all-important thing that unfortunately has to be driven through the 'resistant sludge' that is society, hence their insistence on clearing away all the social and political pressures that might slow down economic activity.[7] This dominant position reveals firstly the mistaken assumption that the best way to raise the quality of life is to maximise the volume of output for sale, and more importantly an appalling failure to understand that a society is made up of many more elements than its economy and that *if the economy is not carefully controlled it will damage and destroy society.* As Pusey says, '...in the space of only a generation extended family, church, and local community neighbourhood have all been burnt up as fuel in the engine of economic "development"...'[8]

The 'econorats' also illustrate the serious mistake of attending only to cash value. The real economy includes all the factors involved in producing valuable things and experiences and is far wider than that realm in which cash transactions are involved. When these factors are added to the moral, political, social, cultural and ecological considerations which should be taken into account in deciding production, distribution and exchange we can see why Polanyi and others insist that the merely cash economy must be regarded as 'embedded' within the much wider real or 'substantive' economy[9]. To confine discussion just to the cash value of things is actually to ignore most of the real economy.

NOTES

1 M. Bookchin, *The Modern Crisis,* Philadelphia, New Society Publishers, 1986, p79.

2 Susan Hunt, 'The Invention of Scarcity', in *Tranet,* Rangely, Michigan, 1987, p5.

3 E. Schwartz, quoted in H. Daly and J. Cobb, *For the Common Good,* 1989, p17.

4 'Dominique Temple on Economicide', *Interculture,* Winter, January 1988.

5 Polanyi's influential account is given in G. Dalton, (ed.), *Primitive Archaic and Modern Economies; Essays of Karl Polanyi,* New York, Anchor, 1968. See also E. Goldsmith, *The Great U-Turn,* 1988, p65.

6 *Sydney Morning Herald,* 24 Feb. 1992, p9.

7 M. Pusey, *Economic Rationalism in Canberra,* Cambridge, Cambridge University Press, 1991.

8 M. Pusey, *The Impact of Economic Ideas on Public Policy in Canberra,* Public Sector Research Centre, Discussion paper, 10 Oct. 1990, p9.

9 See Dalton, note 5.

9

Profit, interest and unearned income

PERHAPS NO ASPECT of our economic system is less questioned than the right to interest and profit. Before the capitalist era began it was regarded as immoral to receive interest on money but now people who become wealthy this way are admired because they are energetic and/or talented, and in any case '...profits could not be made unless they were supplying people with what they want...'. Those who run profitable businesses are seen to be providing jobs and goods for the rest of society, and doing so more competitively and efficiently than their less profitable rivals. Hence it seems to make sense when governments use tax relief and incentives to encourage people with capital to set up profitable businesses.

Few would see many problems with the 'profits' that are made by small firms owned and run by the people who work in them, so long as these can be regarded as yielding no more than a reasonable income. In the alternative economy outlined in Chapter 12 there could be a large role for 'free enterprise' in this form, with many family businesses and small firms operating to provide useful local services and a satisfactory living to their owner-workers. The major problems arise when we consider profits and interest as forms of 'unearned income' that go to people who have invested money and who receive a return without having to devote any labour to production. This is of course a fundamental component of our economy.

There are two major reasons why we should eventually change to an economy in which interest is not paid on loans or investments. The first is that an economy in which interest accumulates must be a growth economy and it is crucial for sustainability that we develop an economy in which only a constant and low level of producing and consuming is going on. If interest is paid, then the capital in the hands of capitalists increases over time, and because they want to invest all the capital they have there will be constant pressure to build more factories and get people to use up all the things that can be produced.

The second argument is a moral one. Marx was one of many who have insisted that it is wrong that some able bodied people can receive high incomes without having to work for them. Imagine that someone buys a factory and arranges for the manager and workers to go on producing as before. Out of each dollar the firm makes from the sale of its products the workers and managers will normally be paid about 30c. Materials and other production costs will amount to around 55c, and the capitalist will usually take about 10 per cent as profit. Now, it is the labour of the workers and the manager which produces the goods, but they do not get the whole value of what they produced. The owner of the factory takes 10c even though in this case he does no work at all. Therefore you could say he takes that 10c from those who created it.

The sums involved are not negligible. According to one estimate the average profit per worker for all the companies listed on the Australian stock exchange was $6,624 (a little over £3000). This would have been equal to more than one fifth of the average annual income these workers received.[1]

The conventional response here is, 'It takes capital as well as labour to produce goods. Wages are the rewards for those who contribute labour, and interest payments or profits are the rewards to those who contribute capital. After all, if they had not put their capital into setting up a factory there would not have been jobs and goods for us'.

This might sound plausible but only because in our society we allow (almost all) the capital to be owned by a very few people. Of course, if a few have it all, then you have to think about rewarding them to entice them into using it to build factories that will produce things we need. Yet all this would be avoided if the society as a whole owned or controlled all the capital. Ideally, people would put their savings into community-owned banks from which money was lent by locally elected boards whose job was to decide what requests for loans would be most likely to yield benefits to the local society. Then there would be no need to think about enticing the owners of capital to invest in production, and we would not have a situation where at least 10 per cent of society's income goes to the few who own almost all the capital.

The point is that there are ways of organising economic activity whereby capital can be accumulated for investment without giving a small class of people huge incomes for which they do not have to work. Marxists in particular regard it as extremely offensive that most people have to work hard for their incomes, while the capitalist class receives typically very high incomes *without having to do any work at all*. Many who own capital do work, for example in their own firms, but the point is that they also receive incomes from invested capital for which they do not have to work. Most receive dividend cheques from firms in which they have no other role than as providers of capital. Many even leave the investment decisions to managers. Even the dullest can receive an income by leaving his or her money in the bank. Yet lots of other people must do work to produce the clothes these people wear and the food they eat. The socialist view is that it is morally wrong that someone can go through life without working while others must work to provide things they consume.

The general socialist solution is simply to have all of society's productive capital — not necessarily property such as homes —owned or controlled by society as a whole. (In Chapter 12 it is argued that most small firms could be privately owned, given the right values.) For instance if all Australia's mines were owned by all Australians as almost all Australia's railways are, then the income (and the losses) would be distributed among all Australians, not just a few.

Socialists believe that labour should be able to earn money but that it is wrong for *money* to be able to earn money. Note that the objection is not to anyone spending their accumulated savings. What socialists object to is the capacity to receive an unearned income in the form of interest on money that has been invested or lent.

If you borrow a surfboard from a friend, what would you think if he or she demanded three surfboards back? However, if you borrow $100,000 from a bank to buy a house you must eventually pay back about $300,000 — and must earn $450,000 to do so, because the tax office takes one-third of your wages. This means that for perhaps five whole years you must work full-time for the banker, who gets $200,000 from your labour without having to do any work for it.

This arrangement is 'normal' in our society; few people see anything disturbing about it. But is there no better way? Why can't money be borrowed and repaid without having to pay any interest at all? This is after all what happens within a good family.

'What about the risk the capitalist takes?'

It is often argued that profit is the reward a capitalist deserves for risking his capital. First, capitalists in general do not lose money. Some do, but on average they increase their wealth every year. The average annual rate of return on investments is often 10–15 per cent. Any capitalist can make money without taking any risk at all by leaving his or her money in the bank. Certainly large numbers of businesses go bankrupt and lose their capital every year, but these are nearly all little people trying to run a corner shop or similar small business.

More importantly, *what is the owner of capital risking?* S/he is risking losing her/his capital, and then having to work for an income like the rest of us! Some risk!

Control as well as ownership

It is also argued that the savings 'ordinary' people have in banks, building societies and pension funds are capital which has been invested and is earning dividend cheques or interest, so what we have is really 'people's capitalism'.

Although there are many people who have small amounts of capital in the bank, almost all capital is owned by a very, few very rich people. Most of the capital that exists is probably owned by 5 per cent of people. However, in addition, these people and their businesses are the ones most able to use the savings the rest of us have in the banks and pension funds. Large firms are more able to borrow these funds. Little people do not borrow many of them, partly because they are not as able to afford the high interest rates, i.e. they cannot afford to bid as much as the big firms for the available finance. So it is important to focus on the ownership *and* control, or use, of capital.

Finally, just consider the enormous number of highly trained people who spend all their time working on all the deals, schemes, transactions and speculations whereby people with money earn more money. Think about all the talent devoted to gambling on currency speculations, working out smart legal moves to secure a takeover, finding new tax dodges or advising people gambling on the stock exchange. Almost all of this effort produces nothing useful to society. Indeed it causes havoc by destabilising currencies and stock markets. Think about what could be done if all that time and energy were sensibly applied to urgent needs.

Banking

There is one area where interest is especially objectionable. When the banks receive a deposit they agree to pay a low rate of interest on it and then lend the deposit out to someone else, who must repay it later at a much higher rate of interest. The person who borrows it uses it to pay for something and the person who sold that item will soon deposit the money back into one of the banks. It will then be lent again to someone else. Depending on the proportion of the bank's deposits the government requires to be lodged in the Reserve Bank, the deposit can be lent out again and again, usually about 8 to 12 times. The bank earns the difference between the interest it must pay to the 12 depositors and the interest it gets from the 12 borrowers.

The only cost to the bank is the labour involved in the bookkeeping required. The above example of the home loan indicates the magnitude of the benefit gained by the bank. If $1 deposited results in a repayment of $3, and it can be lent out 12 times then that initial deposit can result in a $36 income to the banks. Now why should a small number of people be given the right to indulge in this lucrative activity, effectively creating lots of money for themselves at little more expense than is involved in keeping account of the borrowings and lendings? If we are to have a financial system in which loans must be repaid with interest and a dollar deposited can be lent to 12 people at the same time, all of whom are to pay interest on it, then at least the right to lend should only be given to publicly owned banks. Then the vast income from this activity would go to the society as a whole and not to a few private individuals who own banks.

We have now reached the situation where only about 8 per cent of the money in circulation is notes and coin and most is in the form of cheques which are drawn on accounts containing money borrowed from banks. That is, most money involves a debt to the banks; it has been borrowed from a bank and therefore must be repaid with interest. The total debt in most countries is now astronomically big, as are the annual interest payments made to the banks and to the few who have most money to deposit in banks. According to one source, in the late 1980s the US annual interest that had to be paid on all debt was $860 billion, equivalent to about $3600 per person.[2] Another estimate put the 1992 US debt at around $12-13 trillion with an annual repayment bill of approximately $1000 billion.[3] Repayments of capital plus interest on the Third World's debt of $1300 billion come to around $150 billion p.a., three times as much as it receives in all forms of aid.[4] Australia's total debt at the end of 1992 was A\$820 billion (US\$600 billion). Turner estimates that the interest payment (assuming only a 6 per cent interest rate) would have been at least A\$49 billion, or approximately A\$6150 per worker, or more than one fifth of the income half of all income earners receive.[5] Canada's debt in 1991, \$2400 billion, was associated with an interest payment of \$121 billion, equivalent to \$4650 per person p.a.[6] Debt repayments in Canada and in the US were actually around one fifth of GDP! In effect North Americans work one day a week just to pay the interest on debt! (See Note 3.)

Even more remarkable is the rate of increase in debt. Over 30 years from 1962, Canadian real income multiplied by 3.1, but total debt multiplied by 20 and the annual interest payment multiplied by 50. In fact, if that rate of increase in debt continues then by 2020 the entire Canadian GNP would be required each year just to pay the interest on the debt![7] The situation in 'prosperous' Germany is almost as bad. Interest on the government debt has risen four times as fast as the GNP, and would exceed the GNP within 50 years at that rate.[8]

The worst part is that governments go to the private banks to borrow some of the huge sums they need to build dams and railways and they therefore make the taxpayer give billions of dollars in interest to the owners of the banks. '… The Government [of Canada] has to pay as much as 20.8 per cent interest… when the Bank is perfectly capable of creating all the money the Government requires at .35 per cent, as it did in World War 2'.[9] If governments did all their borrowing from government-owned banks they could do so without heaping any interest charges on their projects. The government could borrow the money to build a new dam from its own bank and later when the dam was creating income from the sale of water and electricity the government could simply repay the sum borrowed. This would literally almost cut in half the costs people have to pay for some things, including water. In some years 40 per cent of the income coming into some Australian water boards goes to pay interest to private banks on money borrowed for capital works.[10] In other words, in these instances the banking system ensures that 40 per cent of the amount people pay for their water is siphoned off as income to private bank owners. In the US about 40 per cent of all the money people pay to the Federal government in their taxes is paid by the government to private banks as interest on the government's huge debt.[11]

There have been many occasions when governments have undertaken major developments via government owned banks and therefore without any significant interest payments going to private bank owners. Until recently, the Australian government made many loans at 1 per cent interest to the states for capital works projects. The Sovereignty movement, originating in Canada in the late 1980s, is demanding that governments should never again borrow from private banks.

Is capital a factor of production?

Conventional economics asserts that capital, like labour, is a necessary factor or input for production. It is assumed that without it production cannot take place. Certainly materials, plant and energy are essential for production, but it is a serious mistake to regard capital as a necessary factor, let alone one which deserves a reward for its contribution.

If you agree to help me build a restaurant and in return I agree to give you meals when it is finished, and I make similar arrangements with people who provide bricks and cement, we might build the restaurant without borrowing any capital. Now what has taken place here has been a series of agreements to collect and exchange things needed for the project, and to receive payment later. Where we might have thought we needed capital, we can see that all we needed was organisation; that is, arrangements whereby needed labour and materials could be brought together, used and eventually paid for. When this is done by borrowing money from someone it becomes evident that *capital is really only a power to organise production in a way that extracts wealth for those who provided the money* to get the project underway. The investor who provides the money to purchase the bricks certainly gets the process going but then takes back the investment plus interest. What he has is not anything we must have in order to start producing or building; labour and bricks are the things that make the restaurant, not dollar notes. What he has is the capacity to get production going *in a way that yields income to him.*

In a tribe, a cooperative society, communal village or a genuinely socialist society, no one has this power. People simply discuss and decide rationally what to produce, then arrange for supply of the needed materials and hire of the required workers, paying for these via the community's present or future surplus wealth without any income being siphoned into the pockets of those who possess this mysterious capital 'factor of production'.

In a sane economy we would just discuss whether we had enough bricks, labour and knowledge to build the things we wanted. Our capacity to produce it would not depend on how much money capital people had in their bank accounts. For example, if one night the government secretly added a nought to everyone's bank account, thereby multiplying the nation's money capital tenfold, that would make no difference whatsoever to the country's capacity to build anything.

The ideological force of concepts such as profit and interest should be evident. The belief in the rightness of interest is almost totally dominant and unquestioned. This legitimises a system in which large amounts of wealth constantly pass from the majority who have to work for relatively low incomes to the very few who receive large incomes from interest. A considerable proportion of the amount we pay for everything we buy goes to those who have provided capital for its production. The total interest burden adds up to thousands of dollars or pounds per household per year. Yet virtually none of the majority disadvantaged by the system are calling for its abolition. This is another tribute to the powerful ideological effects of conventional economics.

When capitalists go on strike

Everyone knows about workers' strikes but most have never heard of a strike by capitalists. Yet the owners of capital go on strike when they refuse to invest, or withdraw the money they have previously invested. A capital strike is typically far more damaging than a labour strike. It can close down a factory or a whole industry for good. It can devastate a region or a whole country. Much of the UK is in poor shape with whole cities and industries in decay because capitalists have refused to invest in those regions or industries. Australia's manufacturing industry has declined because owners of capital have withdrawn their capital and reinvested in Asia where wages are much lower. Capital might have remained in those industries, producing things at a profit, but not as high a profit as could be made elsewhere. In a capitalist society capital goes to wherever the highest profit can be made.

The effect has been much more devastating in the Third World, where for 300 years capitalists have been setting up mines and plantations and moving out whenever it suits them. Consequently many large and once very rich areas have been suddenly dumped into squalor. For instance, North-East Brazil once produced vast mineral wealth (which all went to Europe) but is now one of the world's poorest areas.

The conventional view is that, although this is a rather savage way to readjust things, it is important that capital should be free to phase out 'inefficient' ventures and move into more 'productive' ones. The argument is that all will benefit when the capital is used in more efficient new ways. Readjustment from time to time is of course necessary but in our economy the only factors considered are costs and benefits *to those who own the capital.* The fact that thousands of people may lose their jobs or be forced to move out of their communities does not count in the free enterprise economic calculus.

The alternative sketched in Chapter 12 eliminates the possibility that a capital strike could devastate a region, because each region will contain many small farms and enterprises making it highly self-sufficient and therefore able to produce most of the things it needs, even if a big factory nearby were to close. In addition, most of its savings would be in the town bank and lent only to projects that would benefit the town.

So what should we do?

In this economy a considerable proportion of all the work we do ends up in the form of wealth taken by the perhaps 5 per cent of people who own most of the capital. Remember, for each $1 you borrow from them for a housing loan you pay back $3. At least 10 per cent of the price of the things you buy goes as profit to shareholders of the firms that sold them. What's more, profits are 'pyramided'; the costs of that firm include profits taken out by all the firms that contributed to the production of the components in the item sold. For example, when the fridge motor manufacturer buys ball bearings from another company that company's profits are part of the cost to be paid by the motor manufacturer. The cost of the bearings is added to all the other costs of the motor, 10 per cent or more is added on as the motor manufacturer's profit, and the final sum is the cost of the motor to the firm that makes the fridge. But the 10 per cent of the motor's cost included a sum equal to 10 per cent of the profits of the bearing supplier, and when the fridge seller adds 10 per cent to his total cost this will include 10 per cent profit added on by the bearing supplier, and of all the other compounded profits taken out all the way down the line of contributing firms. Hence the proportion of the final price we pay that is profit taken out by various manufacturers would be considerably more than 10 per cent.

As long as the volume of capital to be invested increases through the accumulation of interest there will be a growth economy.

Eventually therefore banks must become places where savings can be safely lodged without earning any interest, and money must be lent by banks interest free. Elected local boards would assess which applicants were most likely to put the loans to the most socially useful purposes given the small amount of investment required for maintenance and innovation.

NOTES

1   Walker, Bob , 'How a water board became a milch cow', Sydney Morning Herald, 23 Feb. 1993, p11.
2   Hixson, J., *A Matter of Interest,* New York, Praeger, 1991, p169.
3   Tanzer, M., 'After RIO', *Monthly Review,* Nov. 1992, p9.
4   Hotson, J., 'Financing sustainable development', Eco-Ed Conference, Toronto, October 1992.
5   *The Economic Reformer,* August 1993, p1.
6   Hotson, *op. cit.,* p4.
7   Hotson, *ibid.* Lower interest rates in the early 1990s have altered the outlook, but not markedly.
8   Kennedy, M., *Interest and Inflation Free Money,* West Germany, Permakultur Publications, 1988. (New edition: Philadelphia, New Society Publishers, 1995.)
9   J. Hotson, 'The Keynesian Revolution', in *Economic Society, 9,* 1987, 185-219.
10 *Sydney Morning Herald,* May 30 1982, p21.
11 J.W. Smith, *The World's Wasted Wealth,* Kalestel, Montana, New Worlds Press, 1989, p215.

The present crisis

THE YEARS BETWEEN 1950 and 1970 saw the most remarkable boom in the 300-year history of our economic system. This was stimulated by the development of more effective communications, transport, shipping and financial networks, the rise of giant transnational corporations and above all the creation of a more unified and integrated world economy. However, since the mid-1970s the economy has entered a period of considerable turmoil and crisis. No one would deny that it is not functioning at all well. Many see it as being in the process of major change, and change for the worse. In most rich countries rates of growth, investment, profits and other indicators have shown a general downward trend for two decades. Within the main industrialised economies, the average annual growth in GNP from 1950 to 1973 was 3.6 per cent. However, from 1973 to 1989 it was only 2.0 per cent. '...the advanced capitalist world has been running out of steam'. There has been '...a narrowing of profitable opportunities for capitalist investment'.[1] World trade has been sluggish and protection is widespread. Real living standards for large numbers have fallen and more people are living in poverty. Effects in the Third World have been much more serious.

This chapter offers an account of the main things happening and the reasons for them. It supports the conclusion that what we are seeing is the increasing incapacity of the present global economic system to solve its problems or to provide for people. Forces built into the foundations of the global economy have inevitably brought about the crisis and we have entered a period in which there will be accelerating decline and damage, probably culminating within decades in the end of the capitalist era.

The drive to accumulate capital

In sharp contrast to the previous era, the essential capitalist idea that became dominant in the west some 300 years ago was investing capital to make more money, not to spend but to invest to make even more, in an endless spiral. In other words, the dominant concern became the drive to accumulate capital to invest and this has been by far the most important factor determining world history over the past three centuries and in determining the nature and destiny of our world today.

Why did Australia lose about half its manufacturing capacity in a mere 10 years? Why is much of the UK in economic decline? Why are millions of Filipino people hungry while half their farmland grows export crops? The underlying reason is that those with capital to invest saw that they could accumulate more by moving manufacturing from Australia, by switching their investment from Britain's north, and by planting Philippine soil with export crops.

Even the rise and fall of nations is primarily due to the quest for wealth by those who own capital. From time to time it suits them to expand abroad and colonise other territories, to withdraw their investment from a country and thereby devastate it, or to promote international hostilities to protect investment opportunities. The role each country comes to have in the highly integrated global economy of the twenty-first century will be the one that promises to maximise the rate of capital accumulation. Although this is not the only factor influencing economic development, it is by far the most important. It explains the present crisis. We must eventually shift to an economic system in which this factor is not allowed to determine our fate.

The crisis: where are we headed?

The drive to accumulate capital increasingly encounters what has been described as the problem of surplus. This can be seen as the fault in capitalism that will do most to bring about the self-destruction of the system. According to the US Bureau of Mines capital is now accumulating in the US at a rate that will see the per capita volume double (in deflated terms) every 20 years. As more capital accumulates, so it becomes more difficult to find profitable investment outlets for it all. Hence there is constant pressure on capitalists and their managers to find new investment fields and new ways of making profits. The phenomena of 'consumer saturation' and 'wealth polarisation' compound the problem. For instance, most people who can afford a fridge already have one, and low income groups are not rapidly becoming more able to do so.

This problem reached a critical level in the 1920s and 1930s, resulting in the Great Depression. This was only solved by the occurrence of World War II which created huge demand for production, thereby soaking up the excess economic capacity in the output of war materials and after the war in the rebuilding of a flattened Europe. But since the 1960s the problem has set in again.

Because it has become more and more difficult for capitalists to invest profitably in producing real objects people might buy, since the mid-1970s investors have increasingly speculated on financial markets and takeovers, to such an extent that this has been called 'the era of casino capitalism'. Debt is an indicator of the nature of the crisis. World debt has exploded in the last 20 years but had it not done so the world economy would have been in far worse shape. Just think how much lower production would have been if the US government had not borrowed so much to pay for it. If the US had made a real effort to balance its budget and reduce its debt the world economy would have plunged into deep depression. Note that the large debt exists at the same time as a huge surplus of capital; the surplus is owned by a handful of the richest banks, companies and individuals, while governments and the rest of us owe the debt to them!

Increasing openness and integration

It is increasingly important to those who control capital to gain access to more markets and regions of the world in which to invest the ever-increasing volumes of capital. Hence, there are powerful tendencies towards 'globalisation', the development of a unified, integrated and deregulated global economy, with all regions open to access by the corporations (although to the present time the unification has taken place within large blocks, such as NAFTA and the EU). They want to be able to sell standardised goods in one big global market, without having to negotiate conditions to enter each national economy in turn, or being unable to enter any regions or lines of business because these have been preserved for local firms. Nor do they want their access to markets to be hindered by tariffs, quotas or other forms of protection. Therefore, governments are under pressure to free the conditions they have previously put on the entry of foreign traders, investors and banks and to enable their countries to become parts of the one integrated and open global market. In the 1980s Australia removed almost all remaining controls over the entry of foreign capital. We are now in a period of major restructuring of national economies in ways that will give businesses greater access to opportunities to buy and sell. One consequence is that individual countries are losing their capacity to control their own economic affairs. The industries they have will mainly be those it suits foreign corporations to locate within their borders. Hence, in Britain and Australia (among many other western countries) we are now highly dependent on imports of many things we produced for ourselves a short time ago. Whether or not we will have enough jobs for our workforce will depend more and more on whether or not it suits foreign corporations to locate plants here. This highly *dependent* situation could only be avoided by strong regulatory and protectionist policies, which clash with the current very dominant free market philosophy.

In two areas these pressures are especially disturbing. One is the move towards a unified global labour market in which wage earners in rich countries will have to compete with labour from the Third World. Corporations are increasingly able to relocate their plants in Third World countries and this will tend to force wages in rich countries down.

Second, the current General Agreement on Tariffs and Trade (GATT) proposals aimed at eliminating protection would make it difficult for a country to block environmentally destructive developments or development jeopardising human rights for fear of being accused of thwarting free trade and having trade penalties imposed. For example, a recent ruling of the GATT declared that the US Marine Mammal Protection Act, designed to protect the dolphin, was an 'unfair trade barrier'. (Global Response, *Newsletter,* undated.) The Act had also banned the sale in the US of tuna caught in nets that kill dolphins and many other species. This ban was attacked under the GATT rules as interfering with free trade and the US was forced to drop it. The implications are extremely alarming as there may now be little a government can do to stop another country or a corporation within its own borders from trading products based on unacceptable safety, health or environmental procedures.

Hence, the constant drive to accumulate capital and to push for more access and better business conditions will make everyone much more vulnerable to the whims of capital. We are in an era of rapid elimination of the capacity of states to protect their citizens from developments that suit big international capital.

Another very important consequence of the crisis has been the pressure from business to have public spending reduced, in order to lower the amount of tax required from corporations. Tax is a cost and the lower the total cost of production the more likely firms can make profitable sales. This is the 'capital comes first syndrome again; governments accept that they '…shou ness to invest and prosper and thus stimulate the econc will benefit everybody'. Those with capital will be less abl   ..nake profitable investments if their taxes are high due to public money being used to support low income or aged people. In the last decade or so governments have cut services, closed down many of their operations (e.g. country railways), sold many government businesses to private owners, and squeezed budgets providing for hospitals, education and poorer people.

In addition, we are constantly told that we must increase our productive efficiency and compete harder, since our country is in debt and only better export performance can lift us back to prosperity. These analysts studiously ignore the fact that all other nations are in debt too, that all are trying to solve their problems in the same export way, and that it is logically impossible for all nations to make money from trade because if one exports more than it imports then others have to import more than they export. All governments are energetically working to facilitate these trends, to reduce their activities and their taxes on the business sector and to open their national economies to international capital. Why? Because they are staffed and advised by people who have learned their conventional economics well! Most governments preside over economies in serious difficulties and the only way conventional economists can hope to 'get the economy going again' is by 'liberalising' their economies, looking for more exports and attracting more foreign investment.

These 'economically rationalist' policies are criticised by people from Keynesian, left, green and social justice origins for not redistributing wealth, 'priming the pump', protecting industries and jobs and allocating more of the nation's wealth to the poor. What these groups usually fail to grasp is that the economic rationalists are taking the only course that the present global economic system leaves open. If governments were to start spending much more on welfare, creating jobs and protecting uncompetitive industries, budget deficits would boom and taxes would have to go up. As a result business costs would rise and profitability and the capacity to employ would fall, and overall economic turnover would decline. Transnational corporations would relocate overseas. Trade competitiveness would suffer. The economic rationalists are quite correct in saying that the old 'big-spending-state' policies would be a disaster, given the integrated and competitive global scene.

They are saying there is now no choice about any of this — *if* you insist on remaining heavily involved in that unified and competitive global capitalist system. You cannot hope to survive in it unless you do cut government expenses and taxes on business, drive wages and welfare down, eliminate protection, devote more resources to exporting, and work and compete more furiously. Only then will you have any hope of being able to earn enough export income to pay for all the imports you need because you removed the barriers which previously preserved your productive capacity, and any hope of attracting corporations to set up and provide us with jobs.

The counter argument from the left or big-state socialist side is that the countries surviving the crisis best are those which have retained much state activity and regulation and have intervened heavily against market forces to help their corporations win in the export competition against other countries. They urge that we should abandon free market dogma and adopt similar policies. The problem here is that this is still only about trying to win in the export scramble when it is only possible for a few to win (and Australia, for example, is not very likely to win, given our high transport costs and wages). It also accepts a highly dependent role for each country heavily integrated into the unified world economy. Above all, it gives no attention whatsoever to any of the problems set by the limits to growth analysis, which indicate that the last thing we need is more exporting.

In unified systems the regions tend to be plundered and abandoned

When localities, cities or states that are relatively independent and self-sufficient economic units start to move into larger and more unified economic systems there can be benefits to the previously separate entities. They can gain more access to distant sources of goods and capital and they might find distant markets for their exports. However it is easy to overlook the very serious disadvantages.

When the town's goods begin to come from more distant businesses, the town begins to lose jobs in the supply of those goods and to lose control over their supply. Buyers can no longer chat to the owners of local bakeries about the qualities of the bread. Whether the town 'prospers' increasingly depends on whether large distant corporations establish plants there. Corporations set up job-creating opportunities in very few towns. Many country towns are rapidly fading. Even when a corporation does come in to establish a plant, a considerable part of the wealth generated flows out of the region, to distant consumers and shareholders.

This is one important reason why alternative economic strategies stress local ownership and local supply; these keep wealth in the town. When people buy goods produced elsewhere money flows out of the town and is therefore not available to pay for things and to create jobs within the town. The distant corporation just comes in to use the town's resources, such as the local mineral deposits or its labour. Unless that labour is willing to work for relatively low wages the corporation will locate somewhere else. Politicians must compete to attract the few corporations, offering them bonanza terms. Most unfortunate is the way that in an integrated economy even the town's savings are taken from it and used (borrowed from the banks where the savings are placed) by distant corporations to develop things far away, rather than things that will benefit the town.[2] Probably the most disastrous effects occur when it suits capital to relocate its activities. When a town has become dependent on a mine or the assembly plant which suddenly closes because the wages in another country are much lower, the town can be ruined.

Only a relatively few regions do well in this centralising and integrating process. The corporations will locate mostly in those regions which promise most return on investment. Those regions will prosper, meaning that there is a powerful tendency for inequality across regions to increase. Clearly those tendencies are contrary to those which would be best for all people, i.e. a development process *which helped all regions to become relatively independent and able to provide jobs and goods for their people secure against the whims of the centre.*

The centralised development vision has become the norm throughout the last hundred years or so. It yields great wealth and power to a very few in the central government and the big corporations and banks, who can then bulldoze a town centre to extend a motorway, or order and pay for a battleship or eliminate an industry. If you value national power and prestige, if you like megabuck developments, if you want an economy in which your country must beat others in competition, then you will endorse this centralist development philosophy. But the wealth and power of the centre is accumulated at the expense of everywhere else. The taxes that pay for the grandiose schemes could have been paid to many local authorities and used to enrich many small communities. There is, in other words, always a contradiction between the centralised development path and local community development. The dominant development philosophy ignores and deprives regions, small towns and suburban communities.

This dichotomy has reached dreadful proportions in the last decade. By some accounts 100,000 towns in Europe are being eliminated, 3000 in Spain alone. The destruction of rural life and country towns in Australia is part of the same phenomenon. This economy does not need little farms and independent towns. Governments and economists eager to get their economies going are facilitating the movement of people from towns to cities. The argument in Chapter 12 is that for many crucial reasons, especially in order to save the ecosystems of the planet, we must develop small local economies, and towns and villages must become the basic units. Yet our present economy is accelerating their destruction.

The social wreckage piles up

We can also understand much of the social breakdown evident in Australia and other rich countries over the last 20 years in terms of the crisis in the global economy. We are experiencing increases in homelessness, drug problems, various forms of crime, family and community dissolution, mental illness, stress-related breakdown, alcoholism and suicide. Rural life is dying out. Our cities and neighbourhoods are much less safe and civilised than they were a generation ago. Why? These are to a considerable extent consequences of the restructuring imposed by capitalism in its ceaseless quest to find more outlets for the investment of ever-accumulating capital. In a global climate where that is increasingly difficult, owners of capital want to adopt the least labour intensive technologies as they are developed; hence unemployment has grown. They also want to be free to locate their operations in the most profitable places and therefore they have moved many of their factories to cheap wage areas overseas. They have pressured governments to remove regulation and lower taxes, which results in reduction in subsidies and assistance to poorer groups, and to many community-maintaining services and functions that help to keep people off the welfare rolls and out of the prisons. Therefore, millions who are old, sick, unemployed or poor have had to get by with fewer resources. Hence the rate of personal, family and social breakdown accelerates. Meanwhile development defined solely in terms of increasing economic turnover is allowed to create urban sprawl and put freeways through settlements and to ignore and harm the subtle social factors that are crucial for establishing community cohesion.

While all this is going on the politicians and economists keep telling us that these cuts and the concessions to business and therefore the transfers of wealth to the rich are necessary in order to get the economy going so that there will be more jobs, more taxes, more to spend on welfare and therefore fewer poor people... when it is those very same policies that are destroying community and creating more poor people.

The system is polarising more and more rapidly. In many countries at least the poorest one-third are getting poorer. In fact some studies suggest that real wages and living standards of most people in western countries have been falling for over a decade.[3] Certainly, inequality increased in the 1980s. On the global scene polarisation is clearly becoming far worse; the poor majority of the world's people are less and less able to pay their way. The important consequence for the global economy is that a large proportion of the world's people are becoming less able to buy all the goods which must be sold if all the accumulated capital is to be invested profitably. Perhaps one-fifth of westerners, and nearly half the world's people, are largely irrelevant to the needs of the global economy or to the interest of the tiny number controlling most of the world's capital. The world economic system will not produce things desperately needed by those countless millions of people, or give them work.

Yet there are abundant resources to solve our problems! For example, if we transferred only about another 5 per cent of national wage and salary income to the poor no people would need to live under the poverty line. The system has made more than 30,000 Australians millionaires, but it decrees that the proportion of national income going to the majority of people must be cut to 'get the economy going again'.

Capitalism has always been characterised by boom and slump. Will we get back onto the good old growth and trickle-down before long? Conventional economists think so but there are some good reasons for believing that this time the system will not recover anything like its old vigour. The global resource and ecological situation is making that more and more implausible. The conditions that underwrote the 1950-1970 boom have gone forever. In general, energy, mineral and biological resources are now expensive and becoming more scarce. Alternative energy sources will have to replace fossil fuels within four decades and they are likely to be *far* more expensive than present energy sources. Most of the ecological costs of production, such as those incurred in dealing with pollution, could be ignored in the 1950s, but cannot be now. Ecological considerations will totally disqualify many resources and practices, and will make others much more costly, especially in view of the rapid loss of cropland, forests and species. Wastes will be more difficult and costly to dispose of. As scarcities increase more people will become incapable of purchasing much, reducing the scope for expanding sales. All this will raise production costs, cut profit margins or raise prices, close off fields of investment and exclude many people from helping to consume all that can be produced.

The paradox of surplus: the more development we have, the more we must have

The problem of surplus, of finding profitable investment outlets for all the ever-increasing capital and productive capacity, is becoming more difficult all the time. Hence the paradox that the more development we have, the more capital accumulates, and therefore the more development and production and consumption there must be in order to enable the ever-accumulating volume of capital to be invested. Not only can we never reach the point in this economy where we are sufficiently developed, but the rate of development must constantly increase.

Two figures drive the point home. In general, productivity (output per hour of work) increases at about 2 per cent p.a., meaning that each 35 years we could cut the work week by half while producing as much as we were at the beginning. (Indeed a number of OECD countries could have cut from a five-day work week *to about a one-day week* in the last 25 years while maintaining their output at the same 1970 level.) In this economy we must therefore double the annual amount we consume per person every 35 years just to prevent unemployment from rising and to avoid a reduction in the productive outlets available to soak up investable capital.

Second, according to the US Bureau of Mines, the amount of capital per person available for investment in the US will increase at 3.6 per cent p.a., i.e. will double in 20 year intervals.[4] This indicates that unless Americans *double* the volume of goods and services they produce and consume *every 20 years* their economy will be in serious difficulties.

In a world where billions are deprived, where the US already uses up far more than its fair share of productive resources and most of the problems are due to overproduction and overconsumption, it would be difficult to imagine anything more absurd than an economy in which the more development there has been the more there must be. Hence the ceaseless and increasing pressure to find more investment outlets, to log more rainforest, to build more tourist hotels, to convert more subsistence farmland to export plantations.

Australia's situation

The crisis in the global economy presents Australia with a grim prospect. We have become heavily dependent on exporting in order to be able to pay for all the things we could produce for ourselves but do not and therefore we have to import. Our main export earners are raw materials and commodities, which have an uncertain future. Of these, our biggest export income earner is coal, consumption of which will have to be drastically limited in view of the greenhouse problem. At the same time we are very dependent on transport and oil, and our oil import bill is likely to be multiplied by *ten* within a decade. Therefore we must now search frantically for the high tech industries that will enable us to beat everyone else in the export scramble. It is very unlikely that we will succeed, given the disadvantage distance sets us and the fact that everyone else is desperately trying to do the same thing in a world glutted with too many unsellable goods!

Even if we succeed, this would just mean that other nations and their workers would lose the sales outlets we won. We are all locked into a zero sum competition for the limited export markets. More businesses could start to win more export orders only if the few who are rich in this world were to increase their already excessive levels of consumption.

But the even greater absurdity is that every nation, no matter how rich and developed, must constantly strive to increase its productivity and competitiveness at the risk of losing the living standards it has built up. We are all on a winner-takes-all treadmill where no one can ever rest, regardless of how developed and powerful their productive systems have become. No country can ever reach a point where effective ways and comfortable living standards have been established and can be guaranteed without any fear of them being lost. In this global economy you are only safe so long as you keep running with the fastest. Unless you are constantly finding new markets, more efficient ways, new things to sell, you will be beaten and trampled.

Australia could long ago have established the infrastructures and industries that would have allowed us to plod along at a relaxed pace producing all we need for very satisfactory living standards without having to concern ourselves much with what was happening in the international economy. We could then have switched our attention to the things that are important in life: artistic pursuits, personal development, learning, community, hobbies or just sitting around and enjoying ourselves, leaving others to scramble for 10 per cent p.a. economic growth as if it mattered. Nothing the predatory global economy could do would then hurt us if we were, as Keynes recommended, producing almost all we needed and only exporting a small amount in order to import the few things it did not suit us to produce. Yet despite a highly talented workforce and vast resources and a GNP per capita *44 times* as high as the poorest half of the world's people, we face economic disaster unless we work and compete much harder! We must desperately seek more export income to pay for imports of food, clothes, furniture, tools, even orange juice from California and of confectionery from South Africa, mostly things which a sane society would not transport across regional boundaries, let alone internationally!

No one in their right mind runs a household economy like this. In your household you have the sense to get production into comfortable and good enough forms and leave it there. Most of us have not changed the way we produce dinners or wash up in years, and our households are not threatened with descent into squalor if we fail to compete against and beat other households in the street. In a sane world it would be possible for a nation to work out ways of doing most things well enough, to develop the infrastructures and industries needed to provide for ourselves most of what we need, and thereafter to have no reason at all to feel threatened by what happens elsewhere or by countries who can produce things more efficiently.

The conventional economists ignore the fact that it is impossible for all trading nations to have a positive balance of trade. If one exports more than it imports then others must have imported more than they exported. The net balance of trade in the world economy must be zero because the volume of exports equals (because it constitutes) the volume of imports. So it is logically impossible for all nations to make lots of money by exporting more than they import. Hence the only point of the export competition game has to be ending up as one of those countries which does manage to earn more in exports than they spend on imports, knowing that if they succeed others must lose. (This does not mean there is no point in trading.)

Again note the absurdity of the current frenzy to increase output, productivity, exports and efficiency, now causing an increase in time spent at work, obliging more women to work for wages, and gearing our 'educational' institutions more and more to purely economic goals, when we could have an economy which provided all we need for very satisfactory living standards on a small fraction of the work we must now do. Many people stick at boring jobs, many work to produce unnecessary and even evil things like weapons, many work hard at getting people to buy more things they do not need, much time and talent goes into doing the accountancy and legal work all this requires, simply because we have an economy in which everyone must find something they can work 35 or 40 hours a week producing or selling if they are to avoid poverty. Yet in a sane economy we might need to work only 10 hours a week or less for a sufficient monetary income and we would be totally secure from the fear that other nations might beat us in the intensely competitive global economy.

Protection

The conventional economist has no doubt that protection is bad. She or he can show elegantly that it makes protected industries inefficient and diverts to them money that consumers could have spent stimulating some other industry. All this is correct but misleading since it takes no account of non-cash considerations nor of the long-term outcomes. There might be important social and ecological reasons why it makes sense to incur the costs of protection, reasons such as keeping communities intact or preserving wilderness. Conventional economists are only interested in dollar effects and proceed as if nothing could ever be as important as 'efficiency'. Now if you think efficiency is the supreme consideration then take off all conceivable protection and assistance to industry and in a short time the few biggest and strongest international suppliers will have taken over the production of everything. They will produce very cheaply but they will have located their plants in Indonesia and Thailand, and your country will have almost no businesses or jobs or capacity to earn export income to pay for imports. This is the way Australia is heading. Our fate will depend on whether we can find something that we can export more efficiently than everyone else.

The conventional economist proceeds as if every country can do this, as if countries will all win the high volume of export sales they *must* win if they are to be able to import the high volume of goods they will not be producing for themselves any more. They do not seem to realise that the last thing likely to happen is an equal or just sharing of the supply of goods or income in the world export market.

It is a fiercely competitive economy in which the few most powerful corporations and nations are working very hard to take export business from everyone else. There are many small nations who are stuck with almost nothing they can export competitively and are unable to invest the sums that might allow them to beat the giants at something. So they have to compete against each other, lowering prices in an effort to sell their few raw materials or labour.

The free market economist is obsessed with the way increasing freedom increases opportunities for profitable business by letting corporations go into fields that were protected or regulated. However, they are indifferent to the fact that when all are free to struggle for the scarce resources, markets and business opportunities, a few of the most powerful will win most of them, with the result that the majority of people and regions will be further deprived. Hence the increasing polarisation in the global economy as the centralisation and free market philosophy grows.

Conventional economists also overlook the fact that the countries that have been most successful in the competition to win export sales have in fact adopted very protectionist policies, with their governments assisting their industries and hindering competitors, most obviously in the case of Japan and the Asian 'Newly Industrialising Countries'.

If your goal is to succeed in the competitive global economy as a country that has allowed itself to become highly dependent on imports and therefore on having to export, then of course you must worry about the undesirable effects of protecting your industries. However, the extensive reliance on protection being recommended here should be seen as part of the total radical conserver strategy detailed in Chapter 12 whereby our high level of self-sufficiency would leave very little need to import and therefore very little need to win export sales. In addition our very low dependence on cash incomes would mean that we would not mind paying considerably more to buy locally made and therefore protected goods, knowing that we were providing for the welfare and security of other local people. Above all, we would be in a situation where our fate depended on our capacity to produce for ourselves most of the things we needed and not on our capacity to beat everyone else at exporting.

Not surprisingly, the current debate about the pros and cons of protection fail to consider this option. That debate is only about whether or not it is acceptable to protect some industries while we are all locked into the struggle to prosper/survive in an integrated and competitive global economy. It makes no reference to the necessary role for many forms of protection built into the concept of highly localised and self-sufficient regional economies.

In the longer run, by urging the abandonment of protection, conventional economists are recommending what most suits the transnational corporations. Reducing protection maximises their capacity to take the sales opportunities potentially available in the world. Because abandoning protection increases economic turnover, to the conventional economist it is by definition a good thing. But the less protection there is the more the world approaches being a single freely competitive arena, a 'level playing field', in which a few elephants will quickly trample all the ants.

Again, this is not to deny that protection involves serious problems of inefficiency, but these ought to be grappled with as political, moral and social problems; they should be dealt with by public debate and action intended to monitor and report on levels of efficiency and to adjust in ways that are best for all concerned.

Conclusions

The argument in this book has been that the global economy does not provide at all well for most people in the world, or for at least one-third in the richest countries, and that the situation will deteriorate in the near future. The economy will take the path that is most likely to maximise profits for big capital. Governments will increasingly assist this, because it is the only way they know to get their national economies going. Hence even though there may be further periods of considerable growth the contradictions are deepening as the years go by. There will almost certainly be increasing polarisation as many more individuals, regions and nations become irrelevant to the global economy.

Developed countries are therefore faced with a stark choice. Either we can go along with the role the global economy prescribes for us, hoping we can edge out some of the other desperate players and find a niche but being increasingly dependent on what suits distant economic forces, or we can largely withdraw from the system and trade only in order to import a few necessities. Of course this would be to accept much lower 'living standards' conventionally defined, but it would mean we could provide for ourselves almost all the things we need for a quite satisfactory quality of life, at our own pace, giving all our people jobs and reasonable incomes, totally secure from whatever insanities the crisis leads the global economy to inflict on itself. No such option is permitted by conventional economic thinking.

NOTES

1   The Editors, 'Globalization – To What End?', in *Monthly Review,* Feb. 1992, pp7–8.
2   Jane Jacobs is one who has stressed the importance of these effects of centralisation; see *Cities and the Wealth of Nations,* Penguin, Harmondsworth, 1986.
3   A. Jamrozik, *Class Inequality and the State,* London, Macmillan, 1991.
4   U.S. Bureau of Mines, *Mineral Facts and Problems,* Washington, 1985, p6.

11

The basic mistakes in conventional economic theory

THE ACCOUNT OF economics found in almost all courses and textbooks is not just open to challenge, it is highly misleading. It leads us to adopt seriously mistaken ideas and practices. The following is a brief discussion of some major faults.

Half the real economy is disregarded

Conventional economic theory concerns itself only with the cash economy and therefore ignores all the production, consumption and investment which goes on continually in any society but does not involve cash exchanges. This includes all the housework, backyard repairs, sewing, shopping, gardening, voluntary work, advice, help and entertainment freely carried out. Housework alone probably accounts for one-quarter of all the work done in our society.[1] Conventional economics regards the breast feeding of infants as of no economic value at all, although it saves a nation millions of dollars in milk that would otherwise have to be purchased at huge resource and environmental cost.

Why do these omissions matter? These important aspects of the real economy are totally ignored in public discussions about how to manage and improve the economy. Consequently governments spend huge sums on strategies to stimulate and adjust the economy, especially through tax relief and subsidies, but almost none of this ever goes to assisting the non-cash sectors of the economy. This means that all the investment subsidies go to the owners of capital or to commercial ventures which benefit from them.

The real economy would be greatly improved if, for example,

people were given subsidies to raise the productive capacity of their backyards. Backyards produce many important things such as leisure services, recreation, entertainment, repairs and vegetables. However, orthodox economic discussions never consider such possibilities because they have been defined as not part of the economy. Indeed, orthodox economic theory would define subsidies for making backyards more useful and enjoyable as consumption expenditure, not investment expenditure, although such expenditure would increase society's capacity to produce many valuable products and services.

Similarly, the many important values that cannot be expressed in dollars are not taken into account in economic decisions, for example the view that would be ruined by building a factory, which is a real cost of its development, or the psychological problems that result when a business closes and retrenches workers. As a result many very important and very real costs of production can be totally ignored by those who should pay them. Economic theory does recognise these costs but refers to them as 'externalities', a term which makes clear that the costs are regarded as not being part of the economy.

Savagely deceptive definitions of 'productivity' and 'efficiency'

The definitions of these two terms are among the most serious faults built into conventional economic theory. These terms simply refer to transactions or arrangements or investments which result in the maximum dollar value of sales and profits. A top Canberra economic bureaucrat recently said that economic rationalism means 'always putting your resources where they will work the best'. He did not mean 'best in view of what is good for people or the environment', he meant 'likely to return most money on the investment of the resources'.[2] As has been stressed above, usually far more profit can be made producing relatively unnecessary things for richer people than producing essential things for lower income receivers. Hence, to the conventional economist investing in one luxury house is a far more 'efficient' and 'productive' use of capital than investing in cheap housing for many poor people. In Britain, hundreds of old people who cannot afford sufficient heating have been reported to die from the cold during a normal winter.[3] Insufficient British capital is invested in producing cheap domestic heating systems, but a great deal of capital is invested in producing armaments, cars and overseas holidays. In many poor countries where people actually starve much capital is invested in producing flowers or strawberries for export to the rich countries. In these cases anyone can see the options in which the available capital should have been invested, but conventional economic theory does not identify these as the most 'productive' and 'efficient' uses. In fact the purposes judged to be the most 'efficient' and 'productive' are often precisely the most wasteful and immoral. Obviously in conventional economic theory the 'efficiency' of an investment has nothing to do with its effectiveness in meeting human need. These definitions mystify and obscure and they legitimise inequality and injustice.

Similarly, when a decision to relocate a plant is made in terms of efficiency only the dollar costs likely for the firm are taken into account by economic theory. The cost represented by the bulldozed landscape or the unemployment suffered where the old plant closed, and the air pollution the factory will generate, are all real and important costs that must be paid by someone. However, they are costs that people other than the owners of the factory have to pay and conventional economic theory enables those building the factory to make the decision about what is most efficient and productive only in terms of the dollar costs they might incur.

How well all this suits the few who own or control most capital! The purposes which make most money for them and which inevitably do least for poor and needy people are spoken of as the most 'efficient' and 'productive'. These definitions help to mislead us into accepting what owners of capital want to do, because we are told that they are only seeking the most 'productive' investments — and we are all in favour of improving 'productivity' and 'efficiency', aren't we?

'Living standards'

This is another very deceptive definition. Most people would agree it is desirable to improve living standards, but a closer look shows that what conventional economists mean when they use this term is merely 'GNP per capita', the amount of production for sale per person. They imply that increasing this raises the quality of life. The relationship between the two is quite problematic. Chapter 4 explained that raising the GNP in a rich country appears not to improve the quality of life, and in fact it can be argued that increasing GNP is now actually reducing our quality of life. Some of the best ways to improve the quality of life would be to develop things which would actually lower GNP, such as edible landscapes to yield free community fruit and community workshops where people could repair things instead of buying new ones.

Surprise, surprise! We again have a definition which suits the owners of capital very nicely. They gain if the volume of sales per person, i.e. 'living standards', increases, even though this might be against the interests of many if not most people. Yet the very term tends to enlist our support.

The Gross National Product

It is not difficult to see why the GNP, the total amount of production for sale, should not be taken as a measure of national wealth, welfare or living standards.

- The GNP only includes cash values; it doesn't count any of the production that is not carried out for money.

- GNP makes no reference to the distribution of wealth or the extent of poverty. Concentrating on whether the GNP has risen ignores the possibility that poverty and hunger have also increased.

- A GNP figure makes no reference to *which* things were produced or consumed. For example, if one country spends a billion dollars on luxuries and nothing on welfare, while another country of the same size spends a billion on welfare and nothing on luxuries, the quality of life experienced in the two is likely to differ greatly. Conventional economic theory has little or no concern with whether the things produced are desirable or necessary; all that matters is that the total volume of production for sale is high, and rising. In other words conventional economic theory is mainly about indiscriminate output and growth and has little interest in what output might be appropriate in view of existing needs. '...An extra dollar's worth of fun for a millionaire counts the same as an extra dollar's worth of food for a starving family with five kids.'[4]

- The GNP includes all the expenditure which actually represents reduction in the national welfare. If you break a window or have a car accident you increase the volume of sales and therefore GNP, even though these outlays arise from events which lower quality of life and reduce national wealth. Much of our national productive effort (possibly 40 per cent according to Hazel Henderson) now goes into repairing damage causing by production, much of which we should have avoided in the first place, such as cleaning up pollution and disposing of excess packaging,

Similarly Daly and Cobb estimate that the US quality of life is falling, meaning that the growth in economic output is going into things like repairing damage caused by other productive activity.[5] A sensible measure of national income would at least separate expenditures representing increases in wealth from those representing reductions in it.

¤ The GNP is only a measure of throughput, that is, the amount spent or consumed each year. It makes no reference to the 'stock' of wealth, its condition, or changes in it. It can be much more important to attend to the wealth of an individual or a nation than to their income if the aim is to estimate genuine economic well-being. Many countries with impressive income figures are piling up huge debts and running down their soils and forests. The US has a vast annual income but that does not mean its economy is in good shape. It is by far the world's most indebted country, its bridges and sewers are crumbling and its soils are depleting rapidly. The US is keeping its income up largely by consuming its financial, resource and ecological capital stock.

The focus on GNP as the only important measure leads us to regard a forest as having no economic value unless it is cut up into logs or woodchips and sold. As we cut it down, GNP increases and that income makes us think we're getting richer, but the loss of the forest means we are really becoming poorer; our capital stock is diminished. The GNP measure encourages us to destroy our stock of ecological wealth by turning it into cash income.

¤ The GNP measure totally ignores the crucial foundations without which the economy and everything else cannot function at all, i.e. the health of our ecosystems. The GNP can be rising as fast as you like but if the soils and the atmosphere and the biodiversity are being damaged our real economic situation, our basic capacity to produce things, is deteriorating. Often the GNP is increased by actions which use up and sell off ecological capital, such as forests. Again, the Index of Sustainable Economic Welfare developed by Daly and Cobb illustrates this contradiction; in the USA it has been falling for 20 years while the GNP has grown. (See Fig. 4.1.)

¤ Finally, it is doubtful whether it makes sense to take much notice of any *single* index of a nation's economic performance. Even a much-revised measure of GNP would still give the impression that all that matters is the volume of cash transactions taking place. It would be much wiser to think about our economy and to compare economies in terms of a profile of many factors, including the degree of inequality, the level of unemployment, the amount of foreign ownership, the costs involved in repairing the damage production is causing, ecological conditions and stocks, and especially the *pattern or form* that the economy's development has led to. For example, how big and how healthy are the cooperative sector, the small business sector, the free goods sector, the domestic sector? Is the pattern, the balance between these and other components, good? When we think about the development of a tadpole we recognise that a fully grown frog is not just a big tadpole. The tadpole develops into a quite different form and ends up with a different ratio of head size to body, etc. Conventional economists have little conception of the development of an economy into a desirable form, and therefore no conception of sufficient development or overdevelopment or warped development. They cannot deal with questions like, 'When will our economy be developed enough, and what form will it take then?' To them, economic development is simply a matter of an economy becoming bigger all the time.

The market myth

As I have explained, the market mechanism does some things well and could have an important place in a satisfactory economy, but it is appallingly bad at allocating goods and determining development according to human need. This is possibly the most serious and inexcusable fault in conventional economic theory and practice. *Market forces are responsible for most of what is wrong on the global economic scene,* including especially the deprivation and poverty, the destruction of community and social bonds, and the destruction of the planet's ecosystems. Above all, if the distribution of goods is left to market forces, the relatively rich few get most of them, the wrong industries are set up in the Third World, and the real needs of many people are ignored. This is because the market attends only to 'effective demand', i.e. to those who can bid most.

You may ask, 'But isn't there a law of supply and demand? When goods become scarce don't prices rise?' This is indeed what happens, if you leave things to a free market among self-interested people, but there are many other ways of organising production, distribution and exchange. Yet conventional economic theory encourages us to believe that there is no other way. However, when things become scarce in a family or in a tribe or a monastery, something very different happens. People then make group decisions about the best way to allocate the scarce resources and they also decide on allocations that attend to needs and that are totally different from those that would result if profit were the determining factor. We could do this in our society as a whole, if we chose to, as many previous societies have done.

Because we have mistakenly assumed that a market is the natural, right and best way, we fail to see clearly the enormous and dreadful moral costs of the market system. The global food market kills tens of thousands of people very day. It allocates food to the rich, even to their animals, and it ignores the desperate need of hundreds of millions of people, because they cannot bid as much as we can for food. If people saw that these are results of our *choice* of the market for the purpose of allocating things, and that the market is not the natural or the best way to allocate many things like food, then we might be more inclined to do something to change these processes. By assuming that economics must be or naturally is about the operation of markets, economic theory helps to obscure this extremely serious moral problem.

The dominant worldview would have us accept that market forces are just about all that matters; the more we leave to the market the better things will be for everyone. But as has been explained the real economy involves much more than market relations; it includes non-cash transactions and in a good society political, moral, religious, traditional and other considerations would also determine production, distribution and investment. Polanyi referred to the way that in most of the societies humans have built the merely market sector of an economy was 'embedded' in the much wider real or 'substantive' economy which included all those other factors and considerations.[6] The more we allow the market to determine what happens, the more the other crucial aspects of a good society are damaged or driven out. In a good society there might be a place for markets but it would have to be a very limited place.

To take the market as the essence of economic activity is of course to endorse the maximum freedom of enterprise. If you have assumed that the market is natural, or that things work best in free markets, then it follows that you should not restrict the freedom of people to bargain in the market place.

Conventional economic theory is only about market economics, not economics in general

Perhaps the biggest deception of all is due to the fact that conventional economic theory is only about the functioning of one specific type of economic system, the free enterprise or market system, yet the principles by which this sort of economy operates are stated as if they are the principles governing all possible economic activity.

For example, we are led to believe that a basic economic law is that if demand increases then price will increase. This is quite true, *in a market economy,* but there have been, and there still are, many other economic systems in which this does not happen. In fact, most types of economy that humans have developed throughout their history have not been at all like ours and have not operated according to principles evident in a market economy (see Chapter 8). There have been and still are many economies in which people produce things and give them to each other. In such an economy there is no concept of bargaining for goods or about prices in a market, nor any notion of individuals competing against each other to get scarce things. There are rules governing exchange and who is to receive various goods. This is in fact the way the Egyptian economy functioned for many hundreds of years, as did the economies of other ancient societies. It seems that only in western society since the sixteenth century has there been the development of an economy in which the market was the dominant factor.

The market economy is merely the particular type of economy we use today, and many very different types of economy are conceivable and have been employed in other times and places.

So it is quite mistaken for economists to proceed as if the principles by which a market economy functions are the basic principles of economics in general. Because they do this we are again given the impression that there is no other sensible or possible way of conducting economic affairs than in the way market systems function. A satisfactory general theory of economics would be based on principles which explain the many varied ways in which societies can produce, distribute, exchange and develop, and the sort of economy that is dominant in the world today would be dealt with as only one of the many different types of economy that the general theory accounted for.

Conventional theory ignores the ecological foundations of the economy

As our discussion of GNP noted, the most important elements in an economy are ecological. What matters most is how productive are the soils, how stable is the climate, how accessible is good water, what are the trends in these factors, and will these systems and processes be in good shape in a hundred years? Trends in the total volume of cash sales not only tell us almost nothing about these crucial factors, but increasing the GNP is what is most likely to damage them by increasing resource demands and the total ecological impact of production.

In conventional economic theory the economy is typically represented by a circular flow diagram of goods and money, unconnected to anything outside the circle. However, the economy should be represented by diagrams which highlight the way material and biological inputs have to come from nature, the state of these stocks, and the fact that the waste outputs must be returned to nature.

Easily overlooked here is the way nature performs many huge tasks for us without any cost, such as replenishing ground water, recycling wastes, keeping the atmosphere stable and the air fit to breathe. As soon as any of these functions begins to falter and we have to try to perform them artificially we immediately run into staggering costs, even to take over a minute part of the task, such as installing water treatment equipment to make a tiny proportion of the globe's once pure water fit to drink again.

One of the most serious consequences of having conceived economic theory solely in terms of cash values is that it has led us into failing to recognise that the basic terms, concepts and laws in a sound economic theory must be ecological. This would give us a very different understanding of things like real wealth and income and it would throw very different light on questions of appropriate investment and distribution. We would then more clearly see how some investments which seem sound in conventional economic terms will actually make us much poorer in terms of our real overall long-term welfare. Some people argue that a satisfactory economic theory would operate in terms of, not dollars, but energy costs and flows.

Distorted and inappropriate development

Because it has been assumed that development is about generating as much economic turnover as possible, the result has been development that is largely inappropriate to the needs of the poor majority. The Third World experience provides the most obvious invalidation of the 'bake a bigger cake' and 'trickle down' premises of the theory.

Appropriate development strategies would make development resources directly available to the majority of people so that they could produce for themselves the goods and services they need. This would conflict head on with the interests of those to whom conventional development strategies make development resources available — that is, the few with capital to invest, and the urban élites with sufficient income to buy consumer products. How very convenient for them that economic theory defines development as promoting maximum possible production for sale!

Growth: the supreme concern

As has been emphasised previously, if there is one principle that is of the utmost importance in conventional economic theory, it is that there should be a constant increase in the amount of economic activity — no matter how high our living standards or the GNP are, and no matter how much overproduction and waste might be taking place.

But as has been explained in some detail, this is the area where conventional economic theory is most seriously mistaken. Not only is the pursuit of growth *not* leading to the solution of our problems, it is now the direct cause of our most serious social and ecological problems.

Capitalists come first in the queue

Conventional economic theory says our economy only works well if and when it suits those who own capital to invest — in other words, if conditions promise good profits for them. Only then will factories be set up and jobs provided and goods produced for the rest of us. Therefore governments are strongly inclined to squeeze the rest of us in order to create a favourable investment climate, i.e. to stimulate more investment activity. The theory doesn't encourage governments to raise wages or pensions; it encourages them to do what will help business prosper.

So the theory raises no challenge to the situation in which a society's productive capacity is in the hands of a few and is put into operation not to produce the things we all need, but to produce what suits the few who own it.

The myth of scarcity

Another way in which conventional economic theory distorts our
thinking is in its assertion that economics is about 'the allocation of
scarce resources among competing wants'. This denies from the start
that it would ever be possible to have established economic arrangements in which there is not a problem of scarcity or in which we have
sufficient production or development.

Many 'primitive' tribes experience little or no scarcity, at least in
normal times. In fact, some anthropologists have described such
tribes as affluent. The Kung Bushmen, for example, only work about
19 hours a week, do not begin to work until they are 23 years old,
spend most of their time socialising and seem to live to a ripe old age.
They undoubtedly enjoy life at least as much as we do and have
virtually no social problems such as crime, even though they live in
a difficult semi-desert environment. All this is possible because the
Kung have simple material wants.[7]

Advocates of the radical conserver society discussed in Chapter 12
insist that we can live cheaply in resource and dollar terms while
actually enhancing our quality of life, if we use only those resources
we need for a comfortable and convenient material lifestyle. This
means wearing things out, repairing, making do with simple, cheap
and durable products, and growing and making many of the things
our local community needs. Most people living in alternative
lifestyles voluntarily and happily live far below the poverty line and
are not interested in consuming more. Given a secure but low
income the issue of scarcity is totally irrelevant to them and it makes
little sense to analyse their economic situation in terms of allocating
scarce resources.

In a well-established conserver society producing all we need for
a very satisfying quality of life would only take a small proportion
of our time. People would easily be able to acquire the relatively
simple goods and appliances that were quite adequate for comfortable and pleasant living. What is more, producing these goods and
meeting our own and other people's daily needs would be sources of
life satisfaction. In this context the concept of scarcity ceases to be
of much relevance to economic thinking or activity. Yet conventional
economic theory makes it central, and therefore works against the
realisation that we could fairly easily achieve a world where scarcity
was not a problem. Again, to define economics as being essentially
about scarcity so that no matter how much we produce, or how

affluent living standards are, we will always have problems deciding what next to spend our incomes on, is to reinforce the world view that suits those who want us to constantly increase the amount of buying we indulge in.

The neglect of power

A notable fault of orthodox economic wisdom is its failure to acknowledge the role of power in economic affairs. In fact, making the free and competitive market the basic concept denies any place for power. Everything is supposed to be determined by market forces which no individual or firm can influence. All are assumed to be 'price takers', meaning that businesses must sell at prices set by the market and cannot affect those prices.

However, virtually all industries are now dominated by a few giant corporations. These monopolies or oligopolies can usually fix the prices and market conditions they want, making invalid the basic premise of conventional economic theory, i.e. *price* competition. Free price competition in the market place determines relatively little to do with the supply or cost of goods, since most prices are to a considerable extent set by the suppliers, i.e. 'administered'. Large corporations can coerce markets, even nations, into accepting their conditions, for instance, by moving large sums of money out of a country, or threatening to close down their operations.

Many of the important economic developments today are decided in deals worked out between government and big corporations, banks, unions and professional or other pressure groups. Economic conditions such as interest rates and wage levels are often determined by a government's response to political action by big corporations, industries and other powerful groups (including unions and environmental and welfare lobbies).

The most important events in the economic world are thus more political than economic. Orthodox economic theory 'depoliticises' these events; it makes them appear to be due to impersonal market forces when in fact they reflect decisions and the exercise of power. Therefore the real subject of study should be *political economy,* not economics.

A society is much more than an economy

As has been emphasised in Chapter 8 a society is made up of many elements besides its economy, such as its political system, community, traditions, cohesion, cultural and religious life, geography and ecology. If we think of the economy as those parts of society that are to do with production, investment, distribution and exchange we realise that only about half of this involves cash, and that within this area it is usually extremely difficult to separate cash factors from others, such as moral considerations. Very often a productive activity results from a complex combination of forces and motives, many of which have nothing to do with cash. For example, try sorting out the purely economic from the moral or affective factors entering into the calculation to feed the family dog. There are monetary costs and benefits involved, such as keeping him in good shape to guard the house, but there are also considerations to do with affection and social expectations. Often the economic aspects of the situation are impossibly 'embedded' in a web of other aspects and it would be absurd to attend only to the economic factors.

Some of the worst effects of conventional economics are due to the way it has come to dominate thinking about social policy. There is a strong tendency to proceed as if all that matters is the cash cost and benefit of different options. In general, social policy should be decided by focusing on implications to do with morality, justice, the quality of life, and the effects on people and places and ecosystems, but these questions are largely ignored in favour of cash-economic considerations; will it pay, will it increase business turnover and the GNP? As has been emphasised, in a good society the focus would be on what is best for the quality of life, the environment and sustainability — and in general this would lead to the adoption of policies which more or less severely restricted the economy. Chapter 5 shows that we would choose to do many things that would prevent the GNP from growing at all, let alone as fast as possible, if our main concern was to do what was moral, just, convivial and likely to contribute most to a high quality of life in an ecologically sound way. Again this is to say that economics, conventionally defined, is relatively unimportant. There are far more important factors that should determine social policy, but conventional economics has hijacked thinking about social policy.

A theory or an ideology?

Again and again we have seen that the definitions or implications of conventional economic theory end up reinforcing ideas which suit those who own capital.

◻ National wealth and welfare and living standards are defined in terms of maximising the amount of production for cash sale.

- ¤ 'Efficiency' and 'productivity' are defined in terms of maximising the return on invested capital.

- ¤ The market is assumed to be the best way or the natural way of organising production and distribution, when it is only one possible way. It is a way which permits capitalists maximum freedom to focus production on the more profitable demand of the higher income groups, thereby seriously depriving most people of goods and services that could have been produced to meet their needs.

- ¤ In other words our economic theory makes freedom of enterprise seem to be the only sensible way to organise economic affairs. Consequently the emphasis is on removing regulation and protection to increase the access and the freedom of opportunity for those who own capital so that they have greater access to the most profitable investment opportunities.

- ¤ Growth is taken for granted as the supreme economic goal which is exactly what those who own the factories would like us to believe. It is not in their interests for economic theory to focus on the fact that we could live very well on far lower levels of economic turnover.

- ¤ Trickle down theory is endorsed; 'Best not to redistribute wealth but to bake a bigger cake for all'. Yet those who are wealthy in the first place get most of the bigger cake produced.

- ¤ Economics is defined in terms which focus on market transactions and which exclude social, moral and political factors. This frees commercial forces from restraint by other than profit and loss considerations.

- ¤ A competitive situation is endorsed (as integral to a market system.) This again legitimises the freedom of corporations to do what suits them and it legitimises the deprivation experienced by the many people who do not succeed in the competitive struggle.

- ¤ Many important but non-dollar costs of production such as environmental impacts are defined as externalities and are therefore easily disregarded.

- ¤ Many costs of production such as travel to work have to be paid by workers and not by employers.

- ¤ The non-cash half of the economy is ignored, which means that all state assistance to the economy goes to the half that produces for sale.

¤ Protection is rejected in principle because it is incompatible with freedom of enterprise and it restricts the amount of economic activity. Again what matters most is increasing the scope for business activity, not protecting jobs or communities from the ravages of the free market.

¤ Capitalists come first in the queue. Not only does 'improving the economy' turn out to mean doing what most suits capitalists, i.e. increasing business turnover, but only if benefits are likely to accrue to them can the rest of us expect benefits.

¤ It makes capital seem like a crucial factor of production, which must be rewarded by interest payments.

¤ Perhaps most important of all, conventional economic theory essentially defines economics only in terms of production for sale, thereby ignoring all the other economies humans have developed, which have not facilitated capitalist access and activity.

It is therefore not surprising that many people regard conventional economic theory as an ideology, i.e. an account which is not just challengeable but which functions in the interests of those who own capital and misleads the rest of us into thinking that what is in their interests is in our interests too. The important questions should be what will do most for human satisfaction and the quality of life, but conventional economic theory has misled us into focusing almost exclusively on what will do most to increase the amount of business turnover.

The 'Ecologically Sustainable Development' (ESD) response

The most common response to these criticisms of economic theory and practice is that while the market model has faults, it is the best one available and that the unfortunate outcomes arise because the conditions economic theory states for markets to work well have not been met. The problem is that in most cases, and for most people in the world, *those conditions never do hold.* What for example, is the good of a mechanism which might allocate things satisfactorily when all participants have sufficient purchasing power to bid, in a world where most people do not? It is at best a neat theory and practice for a world other than the one we live in.

More recently, there has been a response to the criticism that economics fails to deal satisfactorily with environmental problems.

Most of the considerable discussion about 'Ecologically Sustainable Development' falls into this category, as does the influential *Blueprint for a Green Economy*.[8] Hardly any of those contributing to the public discussion of ESD see any need to reject the basic concepts of market forces, the profit motive, the freedom of enterprise or growth. They assume that the main need is to find ways of getting the market to attend to things it does not take into account because they have no cash value ('externalities') — such as ecological costs — so that we can all continue to pursue affluence and growth without harming the environment. Governments are urged to put taxes and prices on scarce items, e.g. taxing fuels according to the amount of carbon dioxide they produce to reduce their use. It is also suggested that they limit the use of some things by granting licences which could be traded between users so that those most able to put them to work efficiently could buy them. More sensible accounting is also recommended, for example to be able to distinguish between production that increases welfare and production that represents reduced wealth (such as car accident repairs).

The first point to emphasise about these devices is that they are interventions contrary to market forces; they can promise to solve the problems only in so far as they bring about actions opposite to those the market would bring about. In other words these are more appropriately seen as regulatory devices to prevent or restore the damage caused by the market rather than ways of getting the market to work well. They are an admission that the market itself cannot solve the problems.

Secondly, these devices do not remedy the distributional consequences of the market, which are responsible for most of the suffering in the world. Indeed, given that the basic market mechanism is to remain as the major determinant of what happens in the economy, these measures will make distributions worse. Limiting supply or raising prices will simply ensure that the items in question will become more scarce and therefore less accessible to ordinary people since they will have to bid harder for them against the rich. The rich will still be able to drive luxury cars and speedboats.

Most importantly, none of these strategies comes to terms with the issue of growth. In the long term sustainability cannot be reconciled with growth. Of course it might be plausible that some regions (e.g. the Third World) and some industries (e.g. solar panels) should continue to grow for a long time and that growth in some service areas might add little to resource use or environmental impact. But if there remains any commitment to continued increase in overall levels of output in the long term then resource and environmental problems (and social problems, see Chapter 8) will move further towards catastrophe.

The limits to growth analysis of our global situation is that there is far too much producing and consuming going on, that per capita living standards, resource use and levels of consumption in rich countries are much higher than all people could have and therefore must be drastically reduced, and that we must move to an economy in which there is zero growth, and in the short term negative growth. All this is completely contrary to the usual ESD rhetoric which assumes that more recycling and energy conservation and environmentally friendly technologies will enable us to solve the environmental problems without any reduction in living standards or any hint that we cannot go on pursuing economic growth. The ESD literature and discussion almost completely ignores the now large limits to growth literature.

Where does this leave economic theory?

It is not easy to understand why current economic theory is so uncritically accepted despite its many obvious and serious faults. Few would claim that it is a conscious plot by people out to deceive us. One factor must be that so many people have a lot to gain by continuing to operate in the existing framework. The business world has a huge demand for economists who will regard economics essentially as a matter of increasing sales. People who see economics that way will get the jobs, and institutions who produce graduates the business world is willing to employ will prosper.

But why do theoreticians still stick to such obviously warped and misleading theory? A major reason is probably that the theory is an elaborate and elegant body of 'knowledge' providing academic economists with a sense of possessing a well-developed discipline and a realm of competence. They would find it disturbing to have to scrap all this and be left without a substantial, respectable, orderly and systematic basis for analysing and teaching. Economists have spent many years learning this trade, becoming familiar with the conventional vocabulary and approach to issues. They would be greatly inconvenienced if they were obliged to move to radically different ways of thinking.

The basic problem is that any realistic alternative theory would either involve the dissolution of economics as a distinct realm of study or its recognition as being quite trivial, depending on how economics is defined. If we take economics as Polanyi urged, that is, as being about everything involved in production, investment, distribution and exchange, then we are going to attend to many factors other than mere cash calculations and we are going to recognise that cash and market aspects of the total economy are 'embedded' in these many moral, social, political and other considerations. We would then have a very difficult and messy area in which what is now thought of as economics would have dissolved into, or become a small part of, the wider field which we might have to label 'human decision making about production, distribution and exchange'. In this field, questions about the dollar cost of things would be relevant but at best of relatively minor significance.

Economics seems neat and manageable now because it selects and deals with only those things that are neat and manageable, namely dollar costs and benefits. If economists focused on the really important questions, such as what is a just price or wage, how best can goods be distributed, what should be developed, what production and distribution arrangements would do most to improve the quality of life, then they would have to grapple with extremely difficult problems involving psychology, philosophy, sociology, morality, ecology and politics. They would frequently have to deal with situations where the most dollar-cheap alternative was not the most morally acceptable alternative, or the most ecologically or socially acceptable.

Conversely, if we were to continue to define economics as being only about cash values, economics would continue to be neat and precise but it would cease to be of much importance, since we would all recognise that almost always there are far more important considerations to take into account. Economists could go on building elegant equations which deal with only dollar variables but economic factors would then at best only be some of those we would take into account in deciding what to produce, how to produce it, and so on.

Economic theory provides one of the best examples of how understanding can be seriously distorted by the reductionism that 'positivist' inquiry risks in its quest for order, especially for order involving quantification. Conventional economics has succumbed to the temptation to attend only to those aspects of economic phenomena that are easily measured, i.e. dollar values. This is like saying that we will only discuss paintings in terms of their lightness or darkness, or that we will use only terms from physics when we discuss what happens in our tennis club meetings. If you take this approach you may be able to make very precise, testable statements and to construct nice mathematical theories but your accounts will be of little value for representing what is really happening or deciding what should be done. You will often mislead and deceive yourself and others because right from the start you will have disqualified yourself from being able to deal with most of the important issues involved, because these cannot be described in the very narrow terms you have limited yourself to.

It is not just that attending only to cash value gives a partial and distorted view of the real economic situation. Conventional economic theory destroys our capacity to see the moral significance of many very important phenomena. We have seen how conventional economics gets us to regard the consequences of the market as somehow natural or acceptable even though on the global scene the market system is responsible for most of the misery, destruction and avoidable death that occurs. Similarly, consider the vast amount of effort that humans put into digging up and refining gold. Only about 5 per cent of gold production goes into industrial or medical uses that are of any benefit to human welfare, the rest is to make expensive and totally unnecessary ornaments for richer people, or for financial speculation. There are gold mines many kilometres deep, employing the talents of highly trained engineers and accountants, whose skills could have been applied to producing things that would benefit people. But conventional economic theory sees nothing objectionable about the efficiency or morality of this stupendous waste of resources.

We have also seen how the economists proceed as if a dollar spent by a millionaire on another luxury is as valuable, as important a contribution to the national wealth, as a dollar spent on something a poor person needs. They also proceed as if there is no significance or economic value in those many real costs and benefits that cannot be given a cash value, such as the misery of unemployment or the boredom of factory work. Because getting the economy going and facilitating as much importing and exporting as possible are held up as the supreme goals, little weight is given in the formation of national policies to the resulting inequality or the experience of urban blight or unemployment or noise pollution. Corporations who win contracts to export garden gnomes to Japan are seen as admirable. Governments are praised for trying to stimulate more consuming and to create more jobs, when there is far too much work and producing and consuming going on. Above all conventional economic theory has led almost all to regard the very thing leading to global catastrophe, economic growth, as the supreme good.

Hence it can be seen why many agree with Bookchin's conclusions on conventional economic theory; '... our present market economy is grossly immoral... the economists have literally 'demoralised' us and turned us into moral cretins.'[9]

NOTES

1   M. Bassand *et.al.*, (eds.), *Self Reliant Development in Europe,* London, Gower, 1986, p207. D. Iremonger, *Households Work,* Sydney, Allen and Unwin, 1988.

2   *Sydney Morning Herald,* 24 Feb. 1992, p9.

3   M. Cooley, *Architect or Bee?* Sydney, Transnational Cooperative, 1980, p65.

4   H. Stretton, *Housing and Government,* Sydney, A.B.C., 1974, p23.

5   H. Daly and J. Cobb, *For The Common Good,* London, Green Print, 1989, pp418–20.

6   G. Dalton (ed.), *Primitive, Ancient and Modern Economies; Essays of Karl Polanyi,* London, Anchor, 1968.

7   K. Sale, *Human Scale,* New York, Coward, McCann, Geogeghan, 1980, p322.

8   D. Pearce, *A Blueprint for a Green Economy,* London, Earthscan, 1989.

9   M. Bookchin, *The Modern Crisis,* Montréal, Black Rose, 1987, p79.

12

The alternative: economics for a radical conserver society[1]

THE FOREGOING CHAPTERS have argued that for many reasons we have no choice but to change to a very different economic system. A glance at the record shows that an economy driven by the profit motive, market forces and the commitment to growth and trickle-down is not solving the big problems. A closer look reveals that these commitments are actually generating a number of the most serious global problems, notably to do with resource scarcity, environmental impact and inappropriate Third World development. Since the early 1970s there has been an increasing flow of literature on the need for an alternative economics. The argument in this final chapter is that there is only one general alternative open to us.

The three most important sources of our problems are growth, the market and production for profit. Previous chapters have shown how these inevitably waste resources and labour, deprive the poor, distribute output badly, fail to produce the most needed things, and provide for most people only via the extremely inefficient and unjust trickle-down process. We need an economic system in which what is done is what is best for humans and the environment, not what is most profitable or what promotes maximum business activity.

Now if capitalist free enterprise is the problem, is socialism or communism the answer? There should be no doubt that the economies that are usually referred to by these terms are definitely not the answer. The Soviet Union and various western countries have practised 'big-state' forms of socialism involving massive, centralised, heavy-handed bureaucracies, a minimum of initiative and responsibility on the part of citizens, and major problems concerning freedom and efficiency. Even more important, they have been obsessed with industrialisation, bigness, endless growth and affluent lifestyles and they have been largely indifferent to the environment.

Yet both the free enterprise way and the centralised big-state socialist or communist way have important merits. We can take something of value from each, but the sustainable and just economy would be so different from these two that we can think in terms of *a Third Way*. Its key elements are inescapably given by the analysis of our global situation.

A sustainable and morally acceptable world order must inescapably be one in which:

◻ *lifestyles are much less affluent:* in other words the GNP is far lower;

◻ there is a high level of household, local and national *self-sufficiency;*

◻ there is much more *cooperation* and sharing; and

◻ there is a *zero-growth* or steady state economy.

Chapter 5 on the limits to growth argued that we in rich countries are living at per capita resource use rates far higher than all people can ever reach, and that cannot be sustained for us for long. The most urgent problems facing our planet cannot be solved unless we greatly reduce our levels of production and consumption. We must therefore shift to an economy in which we can live well yet very simply and in which there is no need to strive endlessly for greater levels of output. It would be appropriate for some selected industries, such as solar panel production, to grow for some time yet. It should be emphasised that living more simply does not imply deprivation or hardship or doing without anything that most people would consider important for a high quality of life. All can have good food, enough warm clothing, a perfectly adequate house and so on, provided our consumption and standards are governed by concern for what is *sufficient* while being as resource cheap as possible.

This means that in the overdeveloped and overconsuming countries the volume of production must be greatly reduced. There must be a long period of negative growth and decline in GNP before we have gone down to 'living standards' — levels of resource use and environmental impact — that all the world's people could have in a sustainable world order. Technically this would not be difficult to do since it is essentially a matter of reducing unnecessary consumption, repairing things, making things last, recycling and changing to less resource-devouring goods, habits and systems.

At all levels from household through neighbourhood, regional and national there would be constant concern to reduce both the amount of unnecessary consumption of non-renewable resources and energy, and the GNP, while increasing the quality of life. Through grants, taxes and penalties, governments would strenuously foster research and development of the most durable and cheap goods and ways of enabling people to live well with a minimum of consuming. Many practices common now would be banned, notably most of what is termed marketing and advertising. Much of the packaging, fashion and magazine industries would cease to exist. Many frivolous and luxurious items would not be produced at all.

Implausible though it might seem at first, a rich country like Britain, Australia or the US could probably provide very satisfactory living standards for all with between one-fifth and one-tenth of the present GNP per capita. It is easy to overlook the many savings in work and resource use that would accumulate if we started to eliminate unnecessary products. For example, if we ceased producing air fresheners, we would save not only the resources used in that product, but we would also reduce the number of trucks needed to transport these products and hence we would reduce accidents, the amount of road wear, the number of warehouses and the insurance required. Our present economy encourages all these unnecessary costs because they all involve increased business turnover and GNP.

A high degree of local self-sufficiency

The essential theme in the economics of a sustainable world must be small-scale and highly self-sufficient social and economic systems. The basic units must be towns, suburbs, local regions and especially neighbourhoods. These must become capable of producing for themselves most of the goods and services they consume, using mostly local sources of land, labour, materials and capital.

A household could easily produce some of its own food, clothing, footwear and furniture, and do many of its own repairs at very low resource, energy and environmental costs. We can build most of our new housing from earth and collect much of our energy and water from our own roofs. We can recycle wastes into the soil by using a garbage gas unit for each five to ten houses. These units would also produce energy to help run our refrigerators. No society can be sustained for long if it fails to recycle food nutrients to the soil.

The neighbourhood economy can easily become greatly enriched by introducing many backyard businesses, small local firms owned

CAN CITIES BE SELF-SUFFICIENT IN FOOD?

• *Home gardens*
One third of the typical house block can feed one person (D. Morris, *The New City States*, 1982, p21.)

• *Idle land*
20 per cent of East Glasgow is unused.
One study of 86 US cities found 2279 square feet of idle land per person. Only 2500 square feet are needed to produce a satisfactory diet for 1 person. (J. Davidson and A. MacEwan, *The Livable City*, 1983, p21.)

• *Unused old buildings*
Possibility one third of all floor space is unlettable.
There are 96,000 acres of vacant houses in UK. (D. Nicholson Lord, *The Greening of the Cities*, 1987.)

• *Flat roofs*
These are a huge desert of unused space in every city. Most could grow vegetables.

• *Parks*
Replace most existing plants with useful trees, shrubs and fish ponds.

• *Other public space*
Hospital and school grounds, space beside railway lines, road verges, nature strips, roundabouts.

• *Dig up unnecessary roads*
Dig up one third of Brisbane's roads and you have 31 square km. of new land.

• *Lawns*
America could produce all its food if it used the land and inputs taken by the lawn. (J. Jeavons, 'The mini-farm' alternative, in *Chicago Tribune*, 17 May 1981, pp43, 47.)

• *Space created by many people who will move to country towns*
Many who live in cities at present will be happy to move out to towns when more of these develop satisfactory local economies.

by those who work in them, and finding or creating local sources of materials for industries, such as clay, cabinet-making timber, animal and plant products.

In addition to extensive backyard vegetable gardening, market gardens should be established throughout suburban areas, on derelict factory sites, beside railway lines and on city roof tops, and where little-used roads can be dug up. These would immediately reduce the cost of food by about 70 per cent because most transport, packaging and marketing costs would be eliminated. We could also establish community gardens in these public spaces. In the Village Homes subdivision of the city of Davis, California about half the planting is of edible and useful species, much of it in public or common areas and beside roads. Imagine how much food your suburb could produce if the plants in the parks and beside the roads were fruit and nut trees. In Village Homes much free fruit is available to all and the area on which 200 houses have been built can produce more than half the food it needs. Indeed it produces more food now than when it was farmland!

The scope for agricultural production in densely settled areas is remarkable. As the accompanying box indicates, in many cities the derelict industrial land alone could almost feed the city. When we decentralise workplaces so that many people can get to work on a bicycle, reduce production so that much less travelling to work is needed in the first place, and produce most things close to where they are needed, we will have dramatically cut the need for vehicles and roads. Many roads can then be dug up and put to food production or other uses.

Most of this urban space can then be developed into permaculture forest-gardens, densely packed with mostly perennial plants so that settlements have permanent self-maintaining sources of food and many inputs for small craft producers.

Tree crops are especially important in this approach. Whereas wheat needs to be planted every year, requiring a tractor to pass over the land many times, flour can be made from many different tree fruits including chestnut, honey locust and carob. The protein content of a number of tree fruits is up to twice that of wheat, and some yields are actually around ten times the yield of wheat per hectare. Some trees can produce five times the fibre yield per hectare that is achievable from a cotton crop. A number of trees actually produce around 100 times as much food per hectare per year as can be derived by using land to produce meat.

Many animals can be included in these systems, especially fish and poultry. These facilitate the recycling of nutrients as well as providing meat, cultivating the soil and controlling pests. For example, ducks eagerly clean up slugs and snails in vegetable gardens.

These sorts of agricultural systems are essential if we are to produce food free from its presently very high energy and transport costs. But there is an even more important reason; they permit nutrients to be returned to the soil. Our present agriculture takes nutrients from the soil and throws them all away. It is not possible to have a sustainable society unless the nutrients are recycled to the soil, and that is not possible unless highly localised agricultural systems are developed, so that food only travels a short distance to households and can then be returned to local gardens, orchards, meadows, woodlots and ponds.

We should establish a community workshop on each block. This would enable us to produce for ourselves many things we now have to buy such as furniture, gifts and toys. It would also serve as a recycling store, library, drop-in centre, surplus exchange, leisure centre, information exchange and committee meeting place.

The alternative or sustainable society literature emphasises that there should be little need to transport basic necessities into local regions, or more than bicycling distance, because there is immense and unrecognised scope for producing most things close to where they will be used, even in the dense city suburbs. We have to move towards the situation wherein the people within a suburb produce from local resources most of the things that are needed to provide the people of that suburb with simple but comfortable living standards. It is probable that a town of only 10,000 people could be more or less self-sufficient in the production of almost all basic requirements.[2] We have to localise production as much as possible around relatively small settlements, if only because it will not be possible to sustain anything like the present volume of importing and transporting of goods.

At the national level the goal should also be far greater self-sufficiency, meaning much less importing and exporting. Australia imports around \$2 billion worth of food each year, although it has no need to import any at all.[3]

Claims like 'Australia can import Brazilian orange juice and sell it more cheaply than Australian juice' are almost never correct. They seem to be true because economists only count the cash costs. The real, total cost of imported orange juice includes the energy used up in transporting it halfway around the world, the materials, energy and labour needed to build the ships, and the damage to the environment from all that activity, especially the atmospheric pollution from the energy consumed. And what about the human costs in hunger suffered by Brazilians whose soils are used to grow oranges

Selected Australian imports 1988-89	
	A$ million
Sauces	22
Pepper	6
Nuts	40
Wine bottle corks	14
Whisky and spirits	148
Orange Juice	33
Cigarette lighters	11
Pens and pencils	50
Wrist watches	90
Toys	150
Clothing and footwear	980

Source: *Sydney Morning Herald,* 31 May 1989, p15

for export rather than crops to eat? When all the real costs are counted, it can be seen that trade should be kept to a relatively few necessities.

Many of the goods produced locally might be dearer in cash terms. The neighbourhood potter cannot make plates as cheaply as the mass-production factory in Indonesia. However, our overall need to buy things will be much reduced and therefore these higher prices will not be so important, especially when we can see that they are enabling local people to be employed providing useful services in an ecologically acceptable way.

Here is a brief summary of where things might be produced.

¤ *From within the household and neighbourhood.* Most water, timber, and recycling of sewage and garbage. Much food, leisure/entertainment, footwear, clothing, and crockery. Much energy from local sources; woodlots, solar panels, windmills, and biomass. Many services, including child minding, care of aged, shared items, skill banks, information, and emergency aid.

¤ *From within the region,* i.e. approximately 10 km. Small firms and cooperatives provide clothing, footwear, appliances, tools, hardware, furniture, bicycles, leisure, finance (local banks), medical services, materials (leather, clay, paint). Some larger regional energy plants.

¤ *From further afield.* A small number of larger factories might supply more complex machinery and specialised materials, from locations spread fairly evenly through the countryside. Perhaps only one national steelworks, car factory, railway equipment producer. Universities, specialised medical services.

¤ *Imported into the country.* Only a small number of complicated or specialised items, e.g. some medical equipment, aircraft, industrial machinery, computer items.

The prospect of developing local economic self-sufficiency might seem unlikely when one thinks about our presently gigantic and dense cities. However, much can be done to make these cities more self sufficient. For example, there are several hundred community gardens in the city of New York. However the recommendations being made in this chapter are mainly intended for a very different settlement pattern, one in which there are many hamlets, small towns and very small cities distributed fairly evenly across the landscape.

The cashless and free sectors

Many people already living in alternative communities have little need for money. Only about 5 per cent of the real income received by people living in an Israeli kibbutz is in the form of cash. In our new economy you would obtain many things from your own garden, or by swapping some surplus produce from your garden or hobby production, or as gifts of surpluses from your neighbours. Whenever you visited the neighbourhood workshop you would find surplus products someone had brought in for anyone to take.

A large sector of the economy would provide totally free goods and services. The fruit growing in the public space in the Village Homes suburb of Davis, California is a good example of this. Our local 'edible landscape' should include many fruit and nut trees, bamboo clumps, woodlots, meadows and ponds from which we can take free food and materials whenever we need them. Similarly, much administration and many services, such as looking after old people and invalids, could be largely performed by people as they go about their daily lives, with little need for cash payments to expensive professionals. We could maintain these sources of free goods by taking part in voluntary community working bees and rosters. This is how many communities look after their commons and free orchards, woodlots, gardens, ponds, workshops and windmills.

These cashless, gift and free sectors of the economy would be extremely important sources of social bonding. Getting things for cash does little or nothing to build gratitude and familiarity. Giving is good for givers and receivers. The more of the real economy we can move out of the cash sector the better. Similar positive effects on solidarity would derive from contributing to the voluntary working bees, committees and rosters that kept our neighbourhood in good shape.

The different sectors of the economy

In our present economy there is increasing pressure to phase out or ignore all but the market sector of the economy. However in a satisfactory and sustainable society the economy would have the following many and varied sectors.

◻ *The free enterprise sector.* This would comprise many small firms, mostly family businesses, owned by those who work in them, operating according to principles of supply and demand but subject to careful monitoring, limits and regulation. Many areas of the economy would not be open to free enterprise. There would be limits on size and types of operations. There would be many small local markets. Some cooperatives would operate as normal trading businesses.

It should be stressed that the free enterprise sector would not be a capitalist sector. People would invest capital in the development of their own business but no one would receive an income just from invested capital. Remember that most capital will exist as savings in town banks with elected boards which lend to worthwhile purposes, or take the form of credit that the government's banks can create to lend to socially valuable ventures or development projects.

◻ *Social planning of basic options.* Mostly discussion at the town level would decide basic investment, development, and distribution issues for the locality. There would be few large businesses, such as railways or steel works, run by public agencies. Community Development Corporations, town banks and business incubators would determine local development after extensive public discussion.

◻ *The cooperative sector.* Many local cooperatives would attend to provision of many goods and services, some operating outside the cash sector.

◻ *The financial sector.* Provision of finance would be via public agencies, especially the town bank. Local currencies would exist alongside the national currency.

¤ *A large non-cash sector,* including

- *Barter* and LETS (Local Employment and Trading Systems, whereby people can work for each other and buy and sell things even though they might not have any money, by recording at a central agency the agreed value of their transactions with each other).

- *Gifts and mutual aid.* Giving surpluses away, recycling, giving advice and assistance, contributing to working bees, giving voluntary taxes, patronising local firms and events, using borrowing arrangements.

- *The domestic sector.* Housework, repairs, hobby production, poultry, gardening, entertainment, and teaching.

- *The free goods sector.* This comprises free food and materials from the local edible landscape, recycling stores, skills and information banks, leisure resources, festivals and celebrations, and community. Many free services are voluntarily and informally performed, e.g. contributing to care of children and elderly people.

The overall scope of the economy would be much reduced. We would be producing and consuming much less per capita than we do now, and much of this would have been moved out of the cash sector, making the GNP a small fraction of what it is now. Within the remaining working-for-money part of the economy we would be staffing the hospitals, shops, railways and universities we needed, earning on average only small amounts of money per week and therefore paying only small amounts of tax to the government, which would only need a small income to maintain its much reduced operations. Garbage collection, care of parks, road maintenance, policing etc. would mostly have been taken over by local groups or become unnecessary. That one day a week in which most of us worked for money would be sufficient to provide the much reduced level of goods and services required within the cash sector.

Most tax would be paid to local agencies, not to the federal government. It would then be spent on local development, decided through participatory processes. Because development would mostly be local, there would be relatively little for central governments to spend tax revenue on. However, there would still be national railway networks, universities, courts, postal systems, etc. Non-cash contributions to working bees would be real payments of tax. Some of these could be formalised and recorded, but in a good community much maintenance and development takes place spontaneously, willingly and informally. Often such 'taxation' would be voluntary, and as most would contribute well, a few slackers would not matter much.

Working only one day a week for cash?

If we lived more simply, reduced unnecessary consumption, shifted much production to households and cooperatives and developed the cashless sector, we might need to work in factories or offices for cash only one or two days a week. We would therefore be freed to spend five or six days a week in our gardens, community workshops and neighbourhoods helping produce things for ourselves and others. Those who wanted to work five days a week for money could still do so, but most of us would prefer to spend most of our time working on a variety of activities in our own gardens and on community projects. This would be a much more satisfying work situation than most people experience in industrial societies. One could start and stop when one felt like it, one could control the process and decide how to do the job, one would be working with friends much of the time, and one could see others benefiting from one's contributions. One would own the product and often see it used, and one could exercise many creative skills in much of one's work. We would, in other words, have largely eliminated the huge problem of alienated labour that exists within the factory mode of production. Some of this work might be 'paid' by receipt of the goods produced, or by credit points entitling one to goods and services, but as in a good family, ideally contributions to building and maintaining community facilities would be made willingly without any interest in payment or keeping score.

Many people in alternative communities do work in this way, opting to spend little time working for money because their lifestyles and local economies enable them to get the things they want and to live well without needing much cash. On one settlement I visit, most of the food they need is produced by the voluntary Saturday morning working bees, or exchanged from neighbouring settlements. On some Australian settlements people live very well on about one fifteenth of the national average cash income. One of these people recently said to me, 'We are far too busy to work for money.'

There is no implication here that the role of specialists and professionals would be less than is necessary for good health care, education, etc. Many people would still work full-time in these careers, although many would probably opt to work part-time in

A NORMAL WORKDAY

	IN CONSUMER SOCIETY	IN CONSERVER SOCIETY
7 am	Got up. Breakfast	Got up. Breakfast. Thought out greenhouse plan. Vegetable gardening, Fed hens.
8 am	Travelled to work	Worked in home workshop; fixed chair, helped Mary repair bike. Walked to local library: watched ducks on pond.
9 am	Served customers	On roster at library.
10 am	Served customers	Took home some bamboo stakes from local clump. Helped Fred clean out his fish tank. Pruned roadside berry bushes.
11 am	Coffee in store room	Coffee in garden. Worked out new seed order. Moved goat.
	Served customers	Helped pack nuts in food co-op. Discussed local water catchment plan (we all vote next Saturday).
12 noon	Served customers	On community work roster: painted windmill.
1 pm	Lunch	Sat by stream. Walked home for lunch. Picked salad from garden. Thought out orchard jobs. Discussed problems in drama club.
2 pm	Served customers	Did paid work in local engineering firm.
4 pm	Tea	Had a cuppa in Arthur's pottery
	Served customers	Looked at his new mugs. Arranged another lesson for Mary and me. Helped Arthur mix clay. Brought home two mugs as payment.
5 pm	Travelled home	Bottled plums. Took surplus to neighbourhood workshop. Brought home some surplus carrots Annabel had left there. Browsed through thatching book: we do the goat house roof tomorrow. Chopped wood. Helped Mike shift the bees.
6 pm	Watched TV	Minded kids. Helped Alice read a story. Showed Tim how to divide. Repotted some chestnut seedlings. Watered the garden. Fed animals, collected eggs. Planned energy committee agenda with Dot and Pete. Read a book.
7 pm	Dinner	Discussed tonight's meeting over dinner. Discussed best trees to plant at dam.
	Watched TV	Energy committee meeting at neighbourhood workshop. Played table tennis there. On way home dropped in for chat with old Bill. Sewed slippers by the fire. Discussed jobs for tomorrow.

	CONSUMER SOCIETY	CONSERVER SOCIETY
Jobs done in day	1	Many
Travel to work	1.5 hrs in car	10 mins on foot
Creativity	Little/none	A lot
Variety	Little/none	Heaps
Autonomy	Little/none	Much
Co-operation	Little/none	A lot
Sense of usefulness	Little/none	Much
Control over work	Little/none	Much
Interest in work	Little	Lots
Income	$80	$18 + vegetables + chairs + mugs + slippers + fun + company + ideas + exercise + sense of community…

paid jobs along with the majority of people. The alternative society under discussion involves simplifying and doing many things for ourselves as multi-skilled 'amateurs' (with ready access to professional advice). There are many things that can be done quite well enough in those ways but of course there will always be fields where it does make sense to leave activities to experts.

How much social planning of the economy?

Socialism as it has usually been conceived, where a large state bureaucracy does all the planning, is not a desirable alternative. However, there can be no doubt that in a sustainable and just society there will have to be social control over the basic development, production and distribution decisions. Some things, and possibly many, might best be left to market forces, but we would have to work out ways of publicly discussing and deciding rationally what limits to put on the market, what industries we need to develop, which industries to phase out and how best to relocate their workers, what limits and conditions to put on production and distribution, and which areas should not be planned or controlled.

If we reduce the amount of production and consumption, if cooperatives, small local firms and households carry out much of the remaining production, and if we reorganise so that we need far fewer transport, sewer and water services, then far less bureaucracy will be needed. There will be little to administer and we could carry out much of the administration informally. For example, if our water came from our own roofs, household members could 'administer' their supply systems themselves. The five or ten households using a common garbage gas unit would look after it with no need for a centralised sewer system and its associated bureaucracy. It might make sense to provide for some local inspectors to ensure that health regulations and appropriate designs have been adhered to. The people drawing some of their energy from a neighbourhood windmill or garbage gas unit would have their own voluntary energy committee to look after these systems.

There would have to be some larger and centralised economic planning bureaucracies, for example to work out how to coordinate the national and regional development priorities presently determined by big corporations when they make their investment decisions. The bureaucrats and experts will not make the decisions; they will only analyse and explain the options on which people will probably decide by direct voting. There is nothing wrong with planning, so long as it

A typical neighbourhood at present

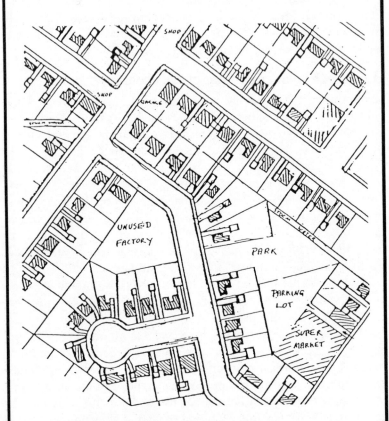

- The car takes 30-40 per cent of the space
- Very little is produced locally: heavy importation of food, clothing, energy, water
- Wastes, especially sewage, have to be transported out
- People have to move out of the neighbourhood to work
- Not much community: lots of isolation and privacy
- No responsibility for running or maintaining the area
- Little or no property owned and run by the community
- Need for high cash incomes, in order to be able to purchase
- A leisure desert
- No free goods, barter or swapping of surpluses
- No working groups or community work groups
- About 80% of us live here

The new neighbourhood

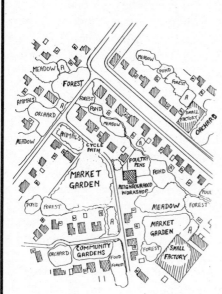

Energy sources
  Windmills
  Solar panels
  Water wheels
  Silicon cells
  Garbage gas
  Woodlots
  Solar ponds
Animals
Industries
  Small firms
  Hobby production
  Co-ops
  Owner-operated
Materials
  Timber, clay, bamboo,
  leather, wool, oils (nut,
  olive), chemicals,
  medicines, water,
  fertiliser, wax
Greenhouses
Home workshops

- Many of the roads dug up and planted
- Most back fences pulled down
- Drains restored to landscaped creeks and ponds
- Derelict factory site has become a market garden
- Supermarket has become a decentralised small firm
- Many small forests, meadows, ponds, orchards, vineyards: some private, some public
- Much property owned and run by the local community, including woodlots, orchards, workshops, housing, libraries
- Most energy sources maintained by local committees
- Many sources of materials
- Many animals throughout the neighbourhood
- Highly self-sufficient in food production, from backyards, local market gardens, and community sources such as orchards, etc.
- Leisure-rich
- A neighbourhood workshop on almost every block
- Many small business, including hobby production
- Many committees to run cooperatives, enterprises, services
- All nutrients recycled to local gardens

is done by us and not by distant bureaucrats. When there is far less to be planned and administered and when most economic activity is devolved into small regions it will be easier for all to discuss and decide the issues. There could and should be a constant stream of referenda enabling us to cast a voluntary vote (either at the town meeting or by telephone code and automatic tallying) on many regional and national issues. This is more or less how many decisions are made in the Swiss cantons.

Community property

The most important 'socialised' parts of the new economy will be made up of the many community facilities and firms that will be owned and run by the community, mostly via voluntary boards elected from local people. There will be many small firms, cooperatives, meeting halls, workshops, libraries, woodlots, ponds, orchards, etc. that are owned, not by the local council but directly by the local community. In many parts of the USA and Europe, Community Land Trusts and Community Development Funds have been formed by ordinary citizens who have decided to pool their savings or secure a grant or use donated land in order to develop the enterprises and facilities they want in their neighbourhood or town. Some have concentrated on buying up housing to keep it available to low-income earners. Some have retained or set up small businesses they believe will make their town more interesting and self-sufficient, even though some of these ventures would not survive in a free enterprise economy. A late 1980s conference of Community Development Funds in the USA was attended by representatives from 35 regions. By the early 1990s more than 2000 of these organisations had generated more than 300,000 low-income housing units and 90,000 jobs within the USA.

These mechanisms make it possible for a community to have its own mini-dairy, beekeeper, shoe repairer, spinner, bakery or pottery, to enrich the town as an interesting place to live and to provide goods and services from local resources and at low environmental cost. In a sound local economy people would buy from the small firms they want to survive even though it would be cheaper to shop at a supermarket. These strategies would build a sense of community, as well as enabling local people to find employment and to derive satisfaction from operating their own small enterprises.

Through these mechanisms we would be catering to the needs of *the whole economy,* and we can see the violence that is done to it if we confine our attention to the merely-cash sector. The whole of the local economy includes all the people who would like a worthwhile job, those who would like to run a useful small business, the satisfaction people get from their jobs, the appearance and convenience of the town, distributional justice, the independence and security of the local economy, the town's spirit and the climate of civility, pride and mutual support, and especially its ecological conditions and the burden the town's imports and consumption are imposing on the global resource budget. If we concentrate only on facilitating the most profitable cash transactions then we will not only overlook the most important parts of the real economy, we will facilitate their destruction.

Crucial for these purposes is the establishment of a town bank, run by an elected board of directors applying a charter which ensures that the savings we put in the bank will only be lent for the development of ventures that enrich the town.

There would continue to be an important role for some large state-owned organisations and for the state provision of some public services that are not easily localised, especially to do with research, the dissemination of new ideas, and the maintenance of health and other standards.

The role of free enterprise

Most economic activity would in a sense be the free enterprise of households, local cooperatives and small firms, all operating within the guidelines set by the overall local economic plan or code. Households could sell surplus eggs and vegetables, or specialise in producing pottery and similar items. Most work for cash could be in small, local, private or cooperative firms producing mostly for local needs, such as the neighbourhood bakery. Small enterprises are often more efficient than big ones. Hence the outstanding merit of a free enterprise economy would be retained; people would be free to set up and run their own projects.

The Briarpatch Network in California is a loose association of small private businesses whose members are not motivated by the desire to make big profits, get rich quick or grow economically. Their goals are to derive personal satisfaction from running their own businesses and providing goods and services which enrich the lives of other people in the local community. If this outlook were the norm then a satisfactory economy might safely involve a large free enterprise sector.

This would also retain the chief merit of a market system which is its capacity to automatically regulate much supply and demand. The scope for the operation of market forces would have to be carefully restricted and monitored but whether or not firms were to sell more or less of many specified items, and at what prices (perhaps within set ranges), could be left to be settled by demands expressed at the shop counter. Most previous socialist/communist experiments have made the mistake of attempting to plan and collectivise everything to do with price, supply, distribution and investment. Few would now argue that this can be done at all satisfactorily.

It would be possible for anyone to set up a new business, for example if they thought they could produce crockery or bread better than the existing suppliers. Town banks might lend the necessary capital if they thought the venture would improve the town. But whether or not the new firm could then put others out of business or whether there was room for all to share the demand would be up to the town to decide, again through its control of credit and purchasing power. People could stop buying from a shop that was putting profit above the welfare of the town. If it seemed best for a supplier to be phased out, in a satisfactory economy the town would work out how best to relocate the people who used to work there into worthwhile activities that those people were happy with. Such specific town development issues would often be on the agenda of town meetings, referenda and public discussions.

'But wouldn't some small firms do better than others and grow and before long wouldn't a few big firms be producing everything again?' This would indeed be the outcome, if getting rich and becoming a tycoon remained a powerful and common motive. Let there be no doubt that whether or not an alternative economy can be achieved depends very much on whether we can shift a long way from those sorts of values. The economic problem is therefore largely a cultural problem. However, the cultural problem is not that enormous; a Briarpatch outlook is all we need.

Nor must we have a complete or sudden change of values before it is possible to start practising the new ways. It will be possible for many firms and communities to start operating without striving to maximise profits or always set the highest price the market will bear even though the mainstream economy still operates according to those principles. As the alternative society develops it will become less and less important for people to maximise their incomes and therefore the pressure to operate according to market forces will diminish. A generation ago there were many small firms and shops whose owners saw themselves as working for a regular income and serving their local communities in a rather relaxed and stable way.

What about big businesses?

There would be far fewer large businesses than there are now, because most would be replaced by small decentralised firms serving their local areas. Nevertheless, some big enterprises such as the railways and a national steelworks would still be needed. Given that eventually we would move to an economy in which no-one receives unearned income, ideally and eventually all firms should be either owned by those who work in them, by community cooperatives, or by society as a whole via the national or regional government (or statutory corporations). The latter would probably run several large enterprises, including the railways. Considerable regulation would be necessary. Supply and demand might partly govern these big firms' activities, but market forces would never be allowed to bankrupt a firm. Some firms would have to be phased out occasionally but again people who work in them and people in the region would be involved in discussions and referenda to monitor efficiency and decide whether to offer the firm assistance in restructuring and transferring workers to other activities.

There would be very few, if any, transnational corporations because there would be a maximum amount of regional self-sufficiency and independence and therefore far less international trade. Big firms would not be allowed to determine major social priorities such as which industries are established where, which plants are closed, and where goods are marketed. Society, as a whole, would make these decisions, again mostly through public debate and referenda. Firms would be given the guidelines within which they were to operate.

Unemployment? None! Automation? No problem!

The essential point to keep in mind about employment is that in a given area there is a certain amount of work that needs to be done to produce what the people there need, and there are a certain number of people who want work or incomes. The task is simply to allocate what needs doing fairly evenly among those who want goods, incomes and work. The market will not do this at all well. It could play a part but there must be deliberate choice and organisation or some people will be unjustly treated.

Because so many of the goods and services used in a suburb or rural area would be produced locally there would always be many interesting and useful things for all to do in the alternative neighbourhood economy. At present much of the work needed to produce the things people in your suburb need is given to people far away, including people in other countries who will work for very low wages. People moving into the neighbourhood could immediately begin working on home production of things to use and surpluses to exchange. They could find out what tasks needed doing in the area; for example, some local small firms might need part-time workers, or the child care cooperative might need more help. They would join in many collective tasks, such as keeping the streets clean or tending community orchards, possibly earning money or credit points for goods and services. Work on some of these tasks might be allocated according to need and it might be paid to some extent from local taxes, to ensure that no one goes without work. Remember that, in general, little paid work would be needed, because people would be able to live simply on low cash incomes.

The distribution of work might be monitored by a (voluntary) local labour coordination committee to decide when adjustments need to be made. It would inform us when seasonal changes required more people for food harvesting or preserving, and it would facilitate the movement of workers, publicising new positions and organising the necessary rosters as changes occurred in the community tasks to be tackled. Generally, it would ensure that all who wanted to work would get a share of what had to be done, so that there would be no unemployment. Many small communities already coordinate all their own work arrangements and have no unemployment. Again the Israeli kibbutz settlements provide an impressive example.

As automation and technical advances reduced the amount of work needed, this committee would coordinate the resulting reduction in work required from all. If the local shoe factory were suddenly automated its workers would be assisted to move to other jobs in the area, while the total work-time needed from all would be reduced. These coordinating functions might require the establishment of some state and perhaps national agencies, for example, to ensure that the distribution of work and the length of the working week were kept approximately equal across various regions.

A more integrated and caring community

At present most of us have little association with other people in our neighbourhood. In the alternative economy we would have a lot more to do with them. It is likely that there would be much more familiarity and mutual concern, because people would be sharing things, swapping, and meeting on committees, working bees, in the workshop and at public discussions of local development issues.

More importantly, they would have a strong interest in contributing to community welfare because it would be important to all people that the local orchards, gardens, windmills, services and so on functioned well. Most people would be in the neighbourhood for most of the week, instead of away at work as they are at present.

This situation would be far more satisfactory for old people, invalids and others with problems because there would be many projects and activities they could join and many people available to talk to and mix with. Handicapped and old people would be among those to benefit most. There would surely be far less loneliness, crime, drug addiction, stress, suicide, alcoholism, family breakdown and other social problems than at present. These problems result largely from economic hardship and the lack of community. Imagine if some of the resources presently being devoted to bandaiding these problems were instead available to enrich local communities.

Benefiting from the overlaps

Many economic savings could be made by arranging for groups faced with problems to help solve each other's problems. For example boredom is a major problem for old people, and there is a chronic insufficiency of child care. In a sane local economy it would take little effort to arrange for old people to help care for children and thereby derive a sense of making a useful contribution. Similarly we should use garbage to make fertilizer, instead of spending large sums to dispose of garbage and then spending more to produce and import fertilizer. Much leisure activity in a radical conserver society is highly productive, especially via crafts.

Capital, finance, interest and investment

Eventually we must establish an economic system which enables individuals or groups to borrow capital to invest in those ventures in which they are to do the work, but from which no one receives an unearned interest payment or dividend cheque. In a satisfactory economy there would be no unearned income. This is not just a matter of morality and justice. If capital is able to earn interest then we have a growth economy — because the volume of capital will constantly expand and can only be invested if more factories are constantly opened. However, we do not have to undertake a sudden change in this area before we can start building the alternative economy. There are many aspects of the Third Way we can implement now, including many to do with capital and finance.

Capital would be available mainly from suburban or town banks, so that savings accumulated in a region could be invested in producing things to improve the region. Money would be lent to people to invest in worthwhile ventures within the region. The criterion would not be whether the investment would make profits. It would be whether the venture would help raise the quality of life in the area. Even now, governments provide money for community development on these sorts of terms, and 'ethical investment' agencies are starting to do similar things in the private sector. A publicly elected board of directors of our local bank would decide who is to receive loans by reference to a democratically established charter of lending principles based on benefit to the community and not on profit maximisation. Major decisions could be referred to town meetings. The board would make many loans to worthwhile ventures that no normal bank would ever lend to. The town of Maleny in southern Queensland has a 'town bank' operating along these lines, and a 'business incubator' which provides advice, space and secretarial services to approved new small firms.

It should be noted again that because we will be living at much reduced levels of consumption and commercial production, there will be far less need for capital. There will be little need for huge developments such as new international airports, freeways and giant sports stadiums. At the individual level people will not need to borrow much money. There are possibly 100,000 Australians living in relatively simple and self-sufficient ways in alternative communities and on some of these it was still possible in the late 1980s to acquire a share, including access to the benefits of previous development and a building lot, for about $6000, to build a house for $7000, and to live on $30–40 per week. (For details see *The Conserver Society,* especially Chapter 17.) The relatively simple developments needed on some of these settlements are funded by voluntary contributions. The Amish do not have to borrow large sums to pay contractors to put up a barn. They get together and do it themselves.[4]

It should not need to be pointed out that any significant move in the direction of a radical conserver society means the death not only of capitalism but of the growth economy. If people start moving to ways of life and to local forms of economic organisation in which large reductions in levels of production and consumption begin to be made, then the opportunities for the profitable investment of all the ever-expanding volumes of capital in existence would begin to diminish. There is now far more capital and far more productive capacity than we would need in a conserver society. Some of it will be redirected but most of it will just have to be phased out or scrapped. We simply do not need anywhere near as many factories and offices as we have now.

Eventually we will have no interest in the amount of money we earn. This is the situation in many alternative communities at present. People have access to all the things they want, given that their wants are materially simple, and their work is not motivated by income but by the pleasure derived from exercising skills and doing useful things for the community. It will probably be quite some time before this becomes the normal situation and until then there might be an important place for a limited sense of 'profit' as a motivating force. A small worker-owned firm might earn higher income by virtue of its greater effort and efficiency, but this is really a form of wage and is quite different from the receipt of interest on invested capital.

Many regions now have a Local Employment and Trading System (LETS). At Maleny in Queensland the units are not dollars but Bunyas, but no normal money ever changes hands. Such a currency never inflates and the money does not flow out of the town or region. It is possible to have some of one's income in this form and some in dollars, enabling one to pay taxes. Many professionals now receive payment within a LETS.

Thus there is no excuse for the enforced idleness and deprivation that millions of people suffer in times of depression when people with skills remain unemployed and people who need the things those skills could produce remain impoverished merely because none of them has the money to pay for goods or to pay workers. As always the most important level for thinking about what is possible is the community level. A community could arrange for people to help to build things it needs, including businesses, fish ponds, orchards and energy sources, and be paid with bits of paper money printed for the purpose, with which they could buy food etc. Later when the windmill is producing energy people could pay for the energy they received from it with these bits of paper. Other people could exchange the bits of paper they held for normal money at the windmill operators' office, the money for this having been earned by the sale of energy from the new mill. The windmill company would then simply burn the paper money as it comes in. We end up with a windmill paid for without incurring any interest charges and without even having to borrow any normal money to build it. Various towns and regions have financed developments this way.

Standards and innovation

Our present economy provides powerful incentives for firms to keep up standards and to develop new products. In the alternative economy being recommended there would be important problems in these areas. Inefficient firms would not be automatically eliminated by market forces. Whether or not an enterprise was to be restructured or closed down would in general be decided by public discussion about its performance and value. Purely cash measures of efficiency would be minor considerations. Many enterprises would be retained for their social, equity, cultural and ecological benefits.

Remember that we are discussing a way of life in which economic efficiency is not very important. We would not need to buy many things so it would not matter so much if the (well-made, long lasting, energy-efficient, locally-made) fridge cost a lot more than one that could be imported.

There could be many publicly funded agencies concerned to research and develop new and better products, to visit and advise communities regarding possible improvements to their productive and other systems. Where efficiency improvements required reduction in workforces these decisions again should be made through public discussion of possible relocations, not left to market forces.

Remember that many of our present standards are far too 'high'. Our clothes, houses, cars, and holidays are in general too luxurious, elaborate and expensive. In addition we work too hard! (Consider the fact that many shops really only need to be open a few days a week; if you need a new pair of shoes you could buy them on Monday or Thursday.) In a good society we would be much more relaxed and easy going and content with what is sufficient. We would not demand the best. We would be prepared to subsidise and assist others, such as small farming communities, or craft producers, to enable them to enjoy the sort of lifestyle they prefer. If we insist on the cheapest and most efficient production, those people will be swept into unemployment. Such a relaxed, tolerant and caring way is not possible if everything has to be constantly geared to beating all other competitors in the integrated global economy.

The new political situation

The radical conserver society outlined here has been advocated by anarchists for a long time. It is a society in which the people living in an area manage their own political, economic, social and cultural affairs. Because the global predicament demands that we must move to much more decentralised, local and self-sufficient arrangements, it makes sense for people to get together to 'govern' themselves. It makes no sense to have these local economies run from distant, centralised and authoritarian bureaucracies. A very important result would be that *participatory* democracy becomes possible because all people in your neighbourhood or town can be involved in decisions about its development.

Dethroning the economy

In a radical conserver society the economy would be a far less important element in our affairs than it is now. In a sane society we would have only as much economic activity as is needed to provide sufficient, comfortable, secure living standards for all so that we could then devote our energies to other and more important pursuits. (Which is what all 'primitive' tribes do!) We would not even pay for goods or keep any accounts or financial records; we would simply take things from the community stores when we needed them, as people take food or clothes from the family community stores (such as the fridge). This is more or less the way the Israeli kibbutz settlement works.

This means the economy would once more have become 'embedded' in society, as Polanyi explained it had been in other than capitalist societies. Considerations of cash value and gain would not dominate but would be weighed against and often overruled by moral, social, ecological, aesthetic and other factors.

With modern technology, economic activity could become a very minor part of our lives. Surely we could soon carry out all the necessary factory production with one day's work a week per person. By cutting the economy down to sensible size we would give ourselves much more time to spend building better social arrangements, restoring damaged environments, helping less fortunate people, researching interesting scientific problems, exploring our universe, performing plays, practising creative arts and crafts, learning and becoming wiser and better people and simply enjoying life.

Although the transition might take decades to accomplish, there is no obvious reason why we cannot gradually shift from the old to the new economy, by enabling increasing numbers of people to move out of the five day work week, high cash income, high consuming way of life into the more relaxed alternative local economy.

Governments could facilitate the development of alternative economies within the existing growth-and-greed society so that the increasing numbers dumped into unemployment, and those bored in their current jobs, could start to move over to the more sane and rewarding way.

'But it's a step backwards'

When some people first hear about these alternatives they see them as a move against 'progress' and back to a more primitive way of life. Although we must greatly reduce levels of resource use and therefore of production and consumption, this does not mean that we must go backwards in any sense that threatens the *quality* of life.

In the first place many aspects of our present society need not be changed at all. We might retain the legal system, the arts, cultural activities, and many other things more or less as they are now, if we wished to. Secondly, we definitely would not have to give up any of the sophisticated technology or scientific research presently devoted to socially important areas such as health. Our new, decentralised neighbourhoods and towns would have many highly qualified technologists and scientists working to develop the most efficient devices and systems for our local conditions. In fact, we would be able to accelerate research and development on socially useful projects if we stopped wasting talent and resources developing unnecessary products. Just imagine if we transferred the 40 per cent of scientists presently making weapons into developing basic household appliances that would last for decades.

Again it should be emphasised that this vision of a radical conserver economy represents the dissolution of capitalism. No conception of a society in which people live frugally and without economic growth is compatible with capitalism. Therefore the transition under discussion will inevitably be resisted strenuously by those who are desperate to see us adhere to the greed and growth way of life. If the alternative movement can maintain its current trajectory, rapidly gaining acceptance as the failure of the conventional worldview becomes more and more obvious, then the 'revolution' might be won in a remarkably peaceful way, as most corporations simply go bankrupt, unable to sell their merchandise. We will have to be ready to accommodate the flow of unemployed advertising executives and financial advisers as they come across to a more relaxed and useful life in the neighbourhood economy.

The difficult problem of values

This brings us to the most difficult problem of all. The sort of economic arrangements that are possible depend very much on the values that are held. To make a conserver economy work well would require far greater selflessness, mutual concern and social responsibility than exist in any industrial society today. If we are determined to remain as selfish, competitive and greedy as most people are today then there are serious limitations to the change we can make in the economic system. If people remain as obsessed with making profits and getting rich as they now are, if people continue to expect bigger incomes when they do more work or more skilled work, if they continue to regard unearned income as morally acceptable, if they continue to want frivolous luxuries and unnecessarily expensive housing, and above all, if people continue to want endlessly rising living standards, then obviously there's no chance of moving towards the type of economy advocated in this chapter. We cannot build a sane and sustainable economy unless there is enormous value change.

Marx was one of many who have seen this problem. He argued that after the overthrow of capitalism a long period (the 'dictatorship of the proletariat') would be needed during which people would outgrow the old selfish values and replace them with the more humane and caring values needed for a highly cooperative society to work. Many would say that this is the most difficult aspect of the 'revolution'. However, it would seem that we must reverse the sequence Marx assumed; the change to radical conserver insights and values, to a dark green perspective, must take place *before* we are likely to scrap capitalism.

There is considerable evidence that the transition in ideas and values is well under way, although obviously still with a very long way to go. Fortunately, widespread value change is not essential before we can begin to make the transition to a conserver society. We could start moving our suburbs and towns in the required direction by establishing many small firms without any immediate change in the motivation that drives enterprises today. In time, however, as neighbourhoods become more secure and robust communities, concern with income, 'living standards' and growth should diminish and be replaced by values such as desire to participate in community life and to enjoy more leisure, the desire to exercise craft skills and to become a valued citizen and a wiser person.

There are two powerful but easily overlooked factors increasing the likelihood that there will be sufficient value change. The first is the rapidly accelerating rate at which our present society is failing to meet human and ecological needs. It is becoming more and more obvious that the system will not provide for all and that radically different systems and lifestyles must be adopted.

Secondly, the alternative way of life has very strong intrinsic rewards built into it. These are not obvious at first sight, but there can be deep satisfaction in living more simply and self-sufficiently, being part of a strong and caring community, being involved in governing one's region, contributing to the development of sound local economic, social, political, cultural and ecological systems, and having the time and assistance to develop more skills and to grow as a person and a citizen. Those who have had any experience of the alternative way are likely to verify that these can be far more important life satisfactions than can come from the scramble for success in conventional economic terms.

It is most important that more alternative arrangements and more whole alternative communities should be established to make these rewards more visible to all. The more that people can be helped to understand that the alternative way offers a higher quality of life than the conventional way, the more likely it is that the value change will occur more quickly and smoothly than we might have imagined at first. Even at best the transition will take decades, but it *could* be a remarkably quick and nonviolent revolution.

It would be so easy

Before discussing the transition process it should be emphasised that in principle it would be very easy to organise a highly satisfactory economy. Permaculture concepts indicate how any settlement could soon be packed with abundant sources of food and materials requiring little export income to pay for inputs. Most of the things we need for a materially simple but quite adequate lifestyle could come from small local firms. Regions could easily be developed to provide for themselves almost all the resources, goods and services they need. Most of us would not need to work more than a few hours a week for money and our work places could be relaxed and cooperative, and close to home. There need be no unemployment or poverty or insecurity or dependence on the whims of distant corporations, bankers and markets, nor any need to run faster and faster all the time. Our region's development could be entirely under our control, funded by our town banks and determined by participatory decision making.

After all, economics should be simply about people getting together to set up local arrangements to provide the food and clothes and other things they need with a minimum of bother, so that they can then get on with what matters in life. There are many places where eco-villages are being pioneered along these lines.[5] The contrast between this and the path mainstream economics is taking us down is staggering. It asks us to produce and consume voraciously while waiting decades for the benefits of growth maximising strategies to trickle down, even though the record shows that despite fifty years of unprecedented growth almost all our problems are getting worse — yet surely most towns and suburbs could be built into thriving, secure, convivial, participatory and highly self-sufficient economies in less than five years.

A hopelessly utopian vision?

Many would regard the account given in this chapter as attractive but quite unrealistic, because people in general would not be willing to make the changes involved. It might therefore be said that what we need are far less radical proposals which we would have more chance of getting people to accept.

It is important to be clear about the argument here. This book has explained that whether we like it or not, we cannot define a sustainable society other than in terms of the principles discussed in this chapter. We will either make it to a society based on simpler lifestyles, a high level of self-sufficiency, cooperation, and a zero growth economy — or we will not achieve a sustainable society. Whether or not it is unrealistic to ask people in general at this point in time to endorse such a society is not the focal issue. The crucial point is that *we have no choice about these matters;* either we manage to go down the path this chapter advocates, or we will not achieve a sustainable society.

It is not being assumed here that we will take this path. There are very good reasons for thinking that we will not have the collective sense to do so. However I *do* insist that if enough of us wanted to, it would be a very easy path to follow.

Making the transition

Since the 1970s a number of movements and institutions critical of conventional economic theory and practice have emerged, such as the New Economics Foundation and the Human Economy Network. There is a large and growing body of critical literature.

Even more important are the many efforts being made to develop economic systems based on the sorts of principles outlined in this chapter. We can now talk about a loose global eco-village movement, in which many small settlements are attempting to develop their own local economies aimed at meeting the needs of people and their ecosystems and not driven by conventional economic principles.

One focal point of this movement at this stage is on the task of saving dying country towns. As has been noted, a most disturbing consequence of the global economic restructuring taking place is the way people are being stripped from the land and their towns are fading. Following is an indication of the strategy a number of groups such as the US Rocky Mountains Institute are now exploring for enabling these towns to save themselves by breaking their dependence on the predatory national and international economies and becoming more economically self-sufficient. The same general strategy is applicable in the urban setting. (For a more detailed account see Chapter 19 of *The Conserver Society*.)

¤ Form a core group to initiate study and public discussion of the town's situation, resources and goals. Especially important is an analysis of the productive capacity that could be put to providing for the needs of the town, including especially the unemployed and retired people, vacant land, and the capital in various funds and savings accounts that might be transferred to a town development bank or credit union.

¤ Establish community gardens and workshops where people can start to provide some things for themselves and cut their dependence on cash incomes and imports. Organise voluntary working bees to develop the gardens and other 'public works'. Some if not all of the gardening should be cooperative rather than based on private plots.

¤ A most important topic of study is the import and export dependence of the town. What things are being imported that might be made locally? How can local producers of these be helped to get going?

¤ How can living costs be cut, for example by more home production, insulation, recycling, and sharing of surpluses?

¤ Especially important is raising understanding of the need to move to more materially simple lifestyles. Organise to increase the involvement of the townspeople in this process of exploring possibilities. Use doorknock surveys and specific events to collect information on resources available and to encourage involvement.

¤ Establish a LETS and a market day so that people can gain a little cash income from home production or small firms.

¤ Involve unemployed people in these activities from the start. 'Disadvantaged' groups have little reason to expect that conventional economic strategies will ever provide reasonable living standards for them. Their only hope will be via alternative local economic development.

¤ Develop the non-cash sector of the economy as much as possible; the gift and exchange networks, the working bees, cooperatives and the free goods.

¤ Use permaculture principles to develop the region's capacity to provide much food and other materials.

¤ Form cooperatives to undertake necessary functions.

¤ Form a town bank, community development corporation and business incubator. These are crucial devices for enabling the establishment of many little firms that will create jobs and increase the town's independence.

¤ Facilitate craft and homestead skill development to raise self-sufficiency, e.g. skill sharing days, craft clubs, displays, information sources.

¤ Develop local sources of entertainment.

¤ Use voluntary taxes. Those interested might pool some savings to convert a piece of wasteland into an orchard or playground.

¤ Work out how to reinforce town cohesion and solidarity. The town's prospects will be best if all see the importance of getting behind the project.

¤ Develop good community decision-making strategies. How can all be involved in the discussion and the decision-making? Do not expect the council to do everything for us; the project must be highly participatory.

¤ Attempt to establish those few export industries the town needs to enable importation of necessities. Ideally these would be cooperatives.

¤ Hold regular festivals and celebrations.

Two points are of crucial importance. First, it will not be possible to save your town unless most of you are willing to make a considerable effort to support it. That means being willing to buy locally produced goods at higher prices, to accept less sophisticated standards and finishes, and to make your savings available to the town bank at less than the interest rates offered by the national banks. Your local producers cannot compete in prices against the transnational corporations who get their produce from Indonesian factories where the wages are $1 or 50p per day. Similarly you will not have a thriving market day or drama group or edible landscape unless you are willing to be involved and to turn up to working bees. This is the stark choice we have now in the face of a global economy in which corporations are penetrating more and more deeply into every niche, looking for opportunities to take over more business activity. You must get together to work for the survival of your town or it will not survive.

Secondly, there must be no doubt that the purpose of all this is not to find an alternative path to conventional wealth and prosperity for the town or to high 'living standards' for the townspeople. Indeed living standards in normal terms will fall. The goal is to provide conventionally low but sufficient living standards, to build community solidarity and support, to enable all to have a high quality of life, and above all to ensure that the town can survive secure in the knowledge that its fate is in its own hands and that it is not at the mercy of the treacherous and predatory national and international economies.

This has been an outline of the general strategy whereby we might slowly build the new sustainable economy within the old one, enabling more people to come across from the rat race to the more relaxed and humane way. We must initiate it both within country towns and within the more difficult urban situation. If we are lucky then in twenty years or so we might see that we can turn the juggernaut around; that, as conventional ways increasingly fail, people are recognising the sense in moving to the alternative ways that are becoming increasingly visible and available. Anyone concerned to see the emergence of a sane world order can make no more important contribution than to help build new local economies along the lines sketched in this chapter.

NOTES

1 The themes noted in this chapter are explained in greater detail in
   The Conserver Society, London, Zed Books, 1995.
2 K. Sale, *Human Scale,* London, Secker and Warburg, 1980.
3 *The Land,* 6 Dec. 1990.
4 More than 100,000 people live in Amish communities in the USA.
   See D.B. Krabil, *The Riddle of the Amish,* Baltimore, Johns Hopkins
   U.P., 1989.
5 In *Ecovillages Report, and Sustainable Communities,* Seattle, Context
   Institute, 1991.

Why we should be angry: a summary of the faults

H ERE IS A summary list of the faults in our economic system, giving some idea of the magnitude of the cost it inflicts on us.

1 We have to work and earn far too much to pay for things

¤ Probably 20 per cent or more of what we pay for goods goes as profits to shareholders and interest to lenders of capital.

¤ When we pay for things we are paying for their advertising, which can be 25 per cent of the price. Packaging adds similar unnecessary costs.

¤ Many prices we pay are way above the costs of production because suppliers are mostly monopolised, including suppliers of professional services who simply agree among themselves where to set their extravagant fees. Many common items such as car spare parts or spectacle frames are probably priced at 20 times their cost of production.

¤ The costs we pay also include the outrageous fees and salaries that go to the corporation's executives, lawyers and consultants. Almost none of these costs would exist in an economy made up mostly of small, local, worker-owned cooperatives and firms.

¤ The fact that things are not made to last might double the real cost of many items, because they would last much longer if a little extra was spent on design and production.

¤ Goods cost more due to the inefficiency in production that occurs because people do not find their jobs enjoyable and have no incentive to do them quickly or well.

¤ Then there is the huge amount of unnecessary work we have to do because things are organised in resource-expensive ways, such as producing and repairing roads, and trucks to transport food that could have been grown locally. At present more than 70 per cent of the price we pay for food goes to pay these avoidable overheads, especially transport! Add in all the work that goes into repairing avoidable social damage, such as the psychiatric nursing for victims of violence and theft partly caused by unemployment.

¤ It is plausible that the above factors oblige us to work at least 3 times as much as would be necessary in a sane economy — to produce the same material living standards.

¤ Much further reduction in the amount of money we would have to earn would be possible if we took the steps argued for in Chapter 12, e.g. living simply, therefore buying little we do not need, making many things for ourselves, producing many things via local working bees, such as 'free' neighbourhood fruit.

Yet in this economy we must constantly increase production, because capital is constantly accumulating and those who own it want to invest it all profitably. Productivity is increasing at a rate that would enable us to halve the work needed to produce what we need every 35 years, but instead in this economy we must increase the amount we produce and consume, or there is an unemployment problem.

2 This economy is the main factor generating many extremely serious global problems

These include environmental destruction, Third World deprivation, resource scarcity and conflict.

¤ It literally kills tens of thousands of people every day through the deprivation it causes, by ensuring that the food, land, water and other resources around them are devoted to production for others. It ensures that shareholders, managers and workers fight to go on producing arms and ozone destroying gases, because if they do not they will probably be dumped into unemployment and poverty.

¤ It gives us no choice but to consume extravagantly and to increase consumption all the time, because if we do not, the economy threatens to plunge us into recession. Yet we have reached the limits to growth; it is over-production and over-consumption that is causing the planet's serious resource and environmental problems. We are already short of resources and destroying the environment but if we maintain 4 per cent growth for 70 years annual output will be 16 times as big as now, and if all people in the world rise to the per capita income levels the rich countries would have then, world output would be 220 times as great as it is now.

3 Despite making us work much harder than we need to, this economy fails to satisfy many urgent human needs

◻ It produces mountains of wealth but only a few people in the world do very well. Most of the wealth it creates is delivered to the rich. It generates great inequality. Even in the richest countries about 25 per cent of people are materially poor while a few are very rich. This inequality is not being reduced over time despite a *trebling* of real average income per capita since 1945. Polarisation between a small rich group and a large poor group is increasing. Not only is the growth and trickle down strategy extremely wasteful, it is not solving inequality problems as time goes by.

◻ Possibly even more important are the impacts of this economy on social cohesion and the quality of life. For most people in even the richest countries, work has been stripped of meaning and satisfaction by this economy. Our neighbourhoods have been made into dreary dormitories. Our environments are becoming more polluted, noisy and congested. Even those who 'succeed' in the rat race for affluence are likely to experience a spiritual emptiness. Passive consuming is the norm and little citizenship is to be found. Large numbers are unemployed. Many are poor. The profit driven media are dominated by trivia and violence. Increasing commercialisation has undermined social relations and dissolved community. Many suffer loneliness, boredom and alienation. There is therefore a huge cost in crime, depression, alcoholism, drug dependence, violence and mental illness.

◻ The overall situation and outlook seem to be deteriorating all the time. The GNP increases as the years go by, but so do almost all the problems.

Conventional *vs* alternative economics: a summary

CONVENTIONAL ECONOMIC THINKING is overwhelmingly dominant but in recent years it has come increasingly under attack from the new or alternative economics. These pages mostly summarise the alternative view (in **bold** type) about conventional economics.

By far the most important goal is to get as much business going as possible. *The more production and sales and consumption and investment and trade the better.* The more turnover, the more goods for people, and the more jobs, the more taxes for the government to spend on things like welfare.

Conventional economics is *totally indiscriminate*. It does not care what is produced and sold. Much of what is sold is unnecessary, wasteful or luxurious. The rich countries already vastly overproduce, yet the main goal of all their economies is to increase production and consumption as fast as possible. It is very important that the 'overdeveloped' rich countries should greatly reduce their levels of production and consumption; but this is not possible in the present economic system.

Economic growth is unquestionably good; it is the supreme goal. There is never enough producing and consuming going. Keep the GNP rising for ever!

Only increase production of important, needed things to the point where we are producing enough of only those things that

enable us to have a high quality of life on the lowest possible resource use. We must *reduce* total output, production and consumption and arrive at a *zero growth economy*. (This does not mean no innovation or development of new products).

Leave most decisions to the market and to the profit motive. They will best settle problems of how much to supply, what price to sell at, and what to invest in.

> *Plan the basic economic priorities.* Plan to *prevent* much production that would be profitable (e.g. many superfluous luxuries). But some (possibly most) sectors could be left largely to free enterprise and the market, operating within planned guidelines.

The market makes the best economic decisions.

> **The market makes appallingly bad economic decisions!** It does some things well and there could be a role for it. But *it will not allocate a fair share of scarce resources to those in most need;* it always allows the rich to take the lion's share by bidding more. And *the market always produces inappropriate development;* investment goes into industries that produce relatively unnecessary things that richer people want, because this is more profitable.

Free enterprise and the profit motive produce *the most efficient outcomes.*

> This is true only if 'efficient' is defined as the most profitable use of capital. That use is typically not the most moral or socially desirable (because it rarely produces what poor people need).

The best way to enrich all and to solve problems like poverty *is to promote economic growth,* and to generate more national wealth so there will be more jobs and taxes and welfare money for the poor.

> This is the vicious 'trickle down' con trick. Sheer economic growth does result in some benefit for the poor, but *very, very little* in the Third World. Almost all the gain from the

growth and trickle down strategy goes to the richest one third of the people. It is an extremely inefficient and wasteful way to solve the urgent problems of a society. We need more cheap housing and more hospitals, but conventional economics allows those with capital to invest in whatever will maximise their profits (mostly high priced luxury items) so that the government can collect more taxes from this increased wealth... when all that capital could have gone into producing things we need! For example, for each dollar invested in speedboats the government gets about 15c in taxes and therefore has about 4c more to spend on hospitals and welfare housing — when we could have invested the whole dollar in these much needed things! When getting the economy going is the top priority there is a strong tendency to produce the most profitable things, which means what the relatively rich want. Therefore productive capacity and resources are taken out of reach of the poor and delivered to the relatively rich.

Bigness is good. It is good for firms to grow, to expand abroad, to take over others. The bigger the size of firms the more efficient they are.

Smallness is good. Some few things need to be big (e.g. steel works). Very small firms are much better to work in and are more easily controlled by the public. In general firms should only supply their local region, using mostly local inputs.

Interdependence is what we need. Regions and even countries have less and less autonomy. Big foreign corporations and banks control more and more. More capital flows internationally. More trade, more transport.

Independence and regionalism. Make small regional economies (e.g. towns) the basic economic units. Prevent control going to a few big foreign corporations and banks. The *highly self-sufficient regional economy* is the goal, so the people of a given town produce for themselves most of the simple things they need for a high quality of life, using the labour, land, capital and other resources of their region.

We are moving to being *a single integrated global economy.*

Integration means everyone is vulnerable; your fate depends
on what suits some corporate board room in a foreign land. If
they decide to close the subsidiary in your town, the town dies.

*Big centralised corporations and governments operating in an integrated
global economy* mean more efficient production and distribution.
Economies of scale are greater.

In a centralised, integrated economy *resources and wealth are
drained from regions into the centre:* the few big corporations
who can make most profit take all the capital and resources.
This can only be prevented by protecting regions and local
industry. When our town is producing most of what it needs
from local resources we are highly secure. Foreign board
rooms, depressions and stock market crashes can't hurt us.

*Conventional economics harnesses the most powerful motive — individual
gain, profit.* This has built the world we know.

Our individualistic culture has conditioned this motive into
us. In other societies production is motivated by other than
by individual gain. Humans eventually have to replace this
personal gain and greed motive with *(a) willingness to do work
because it is of benefit to their community,* and *(b) enjoyment
derived from doing the work.* This is the motivation for the
work we do in the household economy. It could be quite
difficult to extend it to society in general.

The market restructures effectively. If a firm fails, there is change. If
something is profitable, production of it gears up. A planned
economy can't be anywhere near as efficient.

*This points to the greatest weakness of alternatives to a free enter-
prise economy.* It can be very difficult to get the necessary
changes made; people can resist changes the market would
force upon them. This problem is worse when systems are
big; e.g. in national economic planning. The problem would
be much more manageable if most of the economic planning
was done at the town or neighbourhood level.

Labour is just another factor of production, like bricks or capital. You use it in production according to what will maximise return on investment.

> **Labour should not be treated as just another input** into production. Labour is people. It is all right to leave a brick idle or to scrap it. It is *not* all right to leave a person unemployed and without income. Often we should plan to keep people in jobs even though this would be very inefficient in conventional terms. It is wrong to let profit maximisation result in people being unemployed.

Unemployment is unavoidable; it has to be accepted

> **Unemployment is unnecessary and morally intolerable.** It is an inevitable consequence of this economy, but we should change to an economy that does not have any unemployment. (For example, the Kibbutz economy.)
> If only a limited amount of work is necessary to produce simple but comfortable lifestyles, we should just share it between all who need work. In a sane economy, if someone invents an automated machine there is no problem; we can all increase our leisure a little. But you can only do this in a cooperative economy, not in our competitive one.

It is important to create more jobs.

> **Insane!** We already do *far too much work and producing.* In a sensible economy we would cut production down to what we needed and share the goods and the work. We could then constantly reduce the amount of production and jobs necessary and thus increase leisure time.

Everyone is under constant pressure to find some work to do, to find something new to sell, some new product that can be marketed. Unless you find some way to get into producing something you can't receive an income.

> **This is another of the most serious contradictions in our economy. Far more stuff is produced than is necessary; we don't need anywhere near as much work done as there is now.**

Again, *a sane economy would free us from this terrible drive to produce things,* **because it would enable us to do only that relatively small amount of work needed to supply all we need. The present economy makes us all rush around to find 40 hours work to do each week — when we could all have a high quality of life on perhaps less than half as much.**

Encourage endless increases in greed and consumption. We must not only maintain but constantly increase the level of consumption. Hence it is good to spend tens of billions of dollars every year to advertise; to persuade people to buy and use up lots of things they otherwise would not have bought.

Focus on reducing production and consumption to the point where we just produce enough for very comfortable and satisfactory living standards.

Continued growth is essential for the health of the economy.

The world cannot sustain continual economic growth. **We are already destroying the environment and depleting resources because we are overproducing. And the few in rich countries are already hogging most of the world's resource output. A sustainable economy must be a zero growth economy on far lower per capita levels of output than we have in rich countries now.**
The only reason why we must have growth is because it is a capitalist economy. Those with capital want to invest it to maximise their incomes. At the end of the year they have 10–15% more capital than at the start. They can't invest all this without increasing the total productive capacity of the economy. So there must be constant growth or all the accumulating capital can't be invested and there will be trouble; e.g. depression. This is the most important contradiction in our economy. So we have vast and increasing investment in arms production, trivia, luxuries, speculation on the stock market, etc.

Work is boring for most people. There has to be high division of labour, much hierarchy and bossing. Few can expect to get much satisfaction from their work activity, or any sense of doing something worthwhile for their community.

> **This is one of the greatest disasters our present economy inflicts on us. Most work could be varied (we could do many different things in one day), cooperative, without bosses, under one's own control, interesting, multi-skilled and seen to be doing valuable things for local people. Work could be a most satisfying part of life.**

Economic phenomena are *very important* in society.

> **We should get to the point where economics is *almost irrelevant*, where the few goods and services we need are easily produced on perhaps 5 hours work a week. We could then just take all we need without paying anything. (That's what happens in your household economy.) We could then focus our lives on things like play, learning, hobbies, restoring the environment, and building community.**

The only alternative to a free enterprise or capitalist economy is an authoritarian, dictatorial, planned economy, as happened in the U.S.S.R.

> **Wrong! Alternative/green/conserver economics is opposed to big-state socialism, which existed in the USSR and in Sweden etc. Socialism as we know it is for growth, affluent lifestyles, centralisation, industrialisation and resource-expensive ways... and it adds problems to do with lack of democratic control. We are for small, decentralised, participatory, regionally self-sufficient economies... A Third Way.**

✝

Here lies

THE GROWTH ECONOMY

Died early in the twenty-first century after a long and painful illness.

Once adored by all, eventually despised for breaking so many promises.

Flourished in the days of greed, status and power, but withered when sense prevailed.

Was given to manic-depressive fits and starts; when depressed was prone to trample firms, workers and whole regions.

Finally choked to death, unable to consume all it produced or to reduce consumption to reasonable levels.

Fatal illness — gluttony. Daily consumption reached 50 million barrels of oil, 9,000 tonnes of copper, 13 million tonnes of soil, 40,000 Third World children, $2 billion worth of arms, 40,000 ha of rainforest.

Symptoms: waste, pollution, urban decay, selfishness, apathy, war, poverty, under-development, repression, greed and competition.

Mourned by few
(the few who owned all the capital).

R.I.P.

(REALLY INADEQUATE PERFORMER)

Index

The following pages list books recently published by Envirobook
(Sydney, Australia) and Jon Carpenter (Oxford, UK), the co-
publishers of this book (whose addresses appear on page iv).
Envirobook titles are distributed in the UK by Jon Carpenter.
Jon Carpenter titles are distributed in Australia by Boobook,
PO Box 163, Tea Gardens, NSW 2324.

ALSO PUBLISHED BY ENVIROBOOK, SYDNEY

PLACES NOT SPACES
Placemaking in Australia
Edited by Tamara Winikoff

The concept of 'placemaking' calls for a new way of viewing the
relationship between people and the constructed environment.
This book describes what can happen when people with good
ideas get together. Urban designers, architects, artists,
environmentalists and communities are reshaping spaces into
places.

A variety of experiences is presented from all around Australia,
along with case studies which vary in scale from the revitalisation
of whole towns and suburbs to the design of parks, play spaces and
public art.

Published in conjunction with the Australia Council.

40 col & 30 bw ills. pics.

ISBN 0 85881 138 3   120pp $24.95

TELECOMMUTING
on the information highways
Richard Upton

The information revolution is upon us, and if organisations and individuals are to remain competitive and survive in the years ahead they will have to adapt. Computers and telecommunications make it possible to work from almost anywhere because with Telecommuting it is the work that 'commutes'.

More and more people are choosing to work from home and are exchanging the 'bitumen highway' for the 'information highway'. Why? Because Telecommuting is easier, more productive, and better for the environment – and it gives you more freedom to choose how you want to live.

In this book Richard Upton draws on his extensive experience to provide a clear introduction to the rapidly growing practice of Telecommuting: what it is, how it works, and how you can do it. The book also explains how to decide if you can Telecommute with your job, how to sell the idea to your organisation, and how to create your own home office.

ISBN 0 85881 116 2   124pp $14.95

BEYOND OPTIMISM
A Buddhist political ecology
Ken Jones

"This deep, wise, broad-gauged book combines astute social analysis with invigorating spiritual insight; it clears our hearts and heads for action. Stunningly relevant and rich in both political and contemplative experience, this superb book shatters dichotomies between 'inner' amd 'outer' work — and shows us the wholeness to be found as we take action together to evolve a sustainable civilization."

So writes Joanna Macy about this unique study of the human predicament, underpinned as it is by the persuasive Buddhist combination of radical vision and earthy prgmatism. Ken Jones addresses the spiritual, social, economic and political imperatives as we try and construct a society for the future.

ISBN 1 897766 06 8 224pp £9.99

ANIMAL RIGHTS
Extending the circle of compassion
Mark Gold

The question of animal welfare and rights emerges as one of the great issues of our time, as it forces us to take stock of our place in the created order. A lifelong campaigner himself, Mark Gold offers a challenging account of the aims and achievements of one of the fastest growing reform movements in the developed world.

He also shows how we as individuals can ensure our lives are lived in ways that do not cause animal suffering and cruelty.

ISBN 1 897766 16 5 160pp £7.99

ANOTHER WAY

Positive response to contemporary violence

Adam Curle

One of Britian's leading authorities on the theory and practice of violence and conflict resolution, and an experienced international mediator, Adam Curle has for 25 years out of the last 40 been involved in peace-making efforts in eight wars. He has taught and thought about war from chairs at Harvard and Bradford universities, is a Fellow of the American Academy of Arts and Sciences, and has been nominated for the Nobel Peace Prize.

In this book he shows that although there has always been violence, the post-Cold War trend has been different in both scale and universality. The same is true of gang warfare and violent crime in our great cities. Curle identifies the main cause as alienation brought about by two world wars and their aftermath, coupled with 'decolonisation' in the USSR and Africa, as well as the bewildering social impact of advanced technology. Plus, of course, the legacy of unhappy history.

How can this be opposed? The work of the peace group in the much bombarded Croatian town of Osijek (where Curle has been working) provides a powerful model of how a few local people can change the climate of opinion — despite the opposition of warlords — from rampant militarism to the serious quest for peace. The lessons for international agencies, NGOs and would-be conflict resolvers are clear and cogent.

"A fundamentally positive search for creative and effective ways to peace. Combines a lifetime of experience, study and reflection in seeking a response to contemporary violence." — Paul Rogers, Professor of Peace Studies, University of Bradford

"A succinct historical, social scientific and philosophical explanation of the scope and roots of contemporary violence." — Kevin Clements, Director, Institute of Conflict Analysis and Resolution, George Mason University

ISBN 1 897766 22 X 160pp £11.99